An Iowa Farm Boy's Odyssey:
Priest, Parent, Professor

by
Jim Freiburger

Photographic image on the front cover created by: Inna Horbovtsova
Cover and book design: Beverly A. Hodsdon, Joyce Design Solutions LLC.

Dedication

These pages are dedicated to the people who shared my odyssey,
who live in my memories, every day of my life:
my parents, my brothers, my sisters.

I also dedicate the memoir to those who entered my life later:
my wife Eleanor; my children, Joel and Maria; their spouses,
Lanny and Max; and my grandchildren,
Simon, Sophia, Willem, Emily, and Jackson

Acknowledgments

I gratefully acknowledge all who contributed to the writing of
my memoir. As I began to tell my grandchildren stories about
how my parents and people influenced me, my wife, Eleanor,
encouraged me to write my memoir. She spent endless hours
offering suggestions helping me recreate my past
and our life together.

This story is possible because so many people were there to
support me as I wrote. My son Joel read and made suggestions on
chapters. My daughter Maria encouraged me to read sections of
the book to her family as the story progressed.
And my grandchildren listened to early versions and
motivated me to continue writing.

Leah Williams, coach and editor, both encouraged me to continue
writing and made invaluable suggestions to personalize my story.
Without her support I would never have completed my story.
Mary Boyd made valuable editorial contributions to
early versions of the text.

And finally, my Exeter Writers Group reviewed each chapter,
made constructive suggestions and offered invaluable support.

"Life has no meaning.
Each of us has meaning and we bring it to life.
It is a waste to be asking the question
when you are the answer"

Joseph Campbell

Contents

Some names in this story have been changed.

A Farm Boy and his Dreams: An Odyssey Begins

It Took a Village ...

Priest

Parent

Professor

Freiburger Family Farm then

Award Winning Soil Conservation Strip Cropping Farm
1950

and now...

200 homes, Forest Hills Development

CHAPTER 1

Memory Walk

Memories of the way we were...
Was it so simple then or in the course of time do
we remember only laughter and forget the pain
as we remember the way we were...
(Alan Bergman, Marilyn Bergman, Marvin Hamlisch)

In 2015, I made a pilgrimage of sorts with my wife, daughter, her husband, and grandchildren back to the site of the farm where I grew up. We parked the car on a paved road next to a sign marked "walking path." I looked around and realized I had to create a visual image of a farm now buried under 200 houses, landscaped lawns and meandering asphalt streets. I led the family to the walking path and acting as a tour guide attempted to conjure up memories of a place where I had lived and had my first life experiences 70+ years earlier. I searched the horizon and observed no fences, fields, or tall pine groves around farm buildings. My grandkids saw only suburban houses on that horizon as I attempted to re-create a scene from my past.

Pointing to my right, I began describing the tall pine grove that had lined our lane leading into the farm. I told them how we used to watch the lightning strike the trees and create fireworks-like displays. "My father really loved those trees," I reflected aloud. Once, he had taken a newspaper reporter to the site where one of the tall tamarisks suffered the effects of a thunderstorm. The reporter began his story, "A part of Raphael Freiburger died last night when lightning struck and damaged one of his tamarisk trees."

We continued our walk, and deprived of my youthful surroundings, I probed my memory for images to share. I described paths I'd walked, the wind sweeping sheets of rain across my face chasing cows and herding them home for milking. On Sundays

I hurried the cows because I wanted my parents to get me to the Church early. I had been an altar boy, a special role, and had to put on my cassock to prepare for Mass.

Searching around me for the hills I knew, I saw only rows of walls, roofs. But in the distance beyond the blur of those houses, I visualized green grass shining with an effervescence in the sun; the alfalfa forming waves as the wind swept across the field where I flew my kite and dreamed. I paused wondering how all this changed. Nothing remains of the sites where I flew my kite, but on the path that morning, I was beginning to understand that my dreams had not been simply kite dreams. I searched for words to explain my feelings: I refused to bring my mother to visit the farm site in her waning years. She had had a dream, too, and hers was to keep the farm after my father died in 1985. As she grew older and had to sell, she insisted the buyer keep the farm intact. She was not able to stop the next owner who was not bound by that agreement. That buyer made all the changes. I never talked about the houses on the farm with Mom; it would have pained her.

I think my father would have wept at seeing the houses standing on the land he'd so dearly farmed and treasured. All his dedication of nurturing the soil was now bulldozed and supplanted.

In earlier days I used to hear the spring water flowing and I'd go over to taste its cool freshness after playing in the woods nearby. Not now, the spring had dried up and buried under a wall of earth. It had fed a stream of water for thirsty cows. Now there was not even a cold drink for my grandkids.

I pointed to where tall butternut and walnut trees had cast a long, enveloping shadow and a cool breeze. I gestured toward the top of a hill on my left to show where old craggy apple trees once stood. When the blackberries ripened, my siblings and I would pick buckets of succulent black seedy berries to make jars of jam. Where the original owner's homestead house had stood, only a gouged landscape remained.

I turned toward a new homestead on a nearby hill and thought of another that had stood on top of another hill. It was there that my parents, and six younger siblings and I had eaten, slept, and entertained so many cousins, friends and visitors. I relived with my grandkids the cows bellowing to one another in a patch of woods on my right. The bleating of a new member of the herd had come out of those trees. I had followed the sounds and seen the other cows grazing. Then the calf had called again. I had searched along the line of trees and seen its mother standing at the edge of the woods, checking to see if there was any imminent danger. Then she had brought her newborn out of hiding. Fortunately, I had seen the distant hiding place, or it may have taken some time to find where she had sequestered the little one.

A car horn jolted me into the present moment. The sound made me realize that the current streets and houses had not evolved under the guidance of Mother Nature. Before me I saw a whole world flipped from grass to blacktop.

I walked slowly on the gravel path wondering what memory the next turn might conjure up. I smiled as I saw that our favorite hide and seek patch of woods remained. I had a flashback to my twelfth summer. Marlene Gunther, a visitor my age, with whom we were playing the game in those woods, counted to 50 as my siblings and I scattered to hide. Rather than hide, my brothers Tom, Don and I had run through the trees and snuck home. An hour later Marlene had arrived at the house angry, and shouted, "You thought you could ditch me. But I remembered to look for the house and found my way here." For us it was a common prank; she did not consider it a gesture of hospitality.

On my right, I saw a newly landscaped terrace. I remembered the savvy cows had created curved paths on that same hill so they could walk on level ground and avoid a steep climb. We had lived on our farm several years before my father discovered the cows' secret, and following their example, he designed these same contours in his fields. He was the first in our area to find this secret. He had worked with the Soil Conservation Service to lay out the fields in "strip cropping." He not only copied the cows contouring the hills but prevented the topsoil from washing away. I watched, wistfully, as my grandkids tried to create their own winding paths, imagining the cows routinely following the earthen tracks they had created.

Their hillside gazes brought back another memory. Some of the cows had discovered that leaning over the fence at the top of that hill yielded ears of corn hanging on the stalks. I described how we had hung ears of corn on an electric fence wire to stop the cows' thievery. A controller had been attached to the wire. Every two seconds an electric surge had passed along the wire. After tying an ear of corn to the wire, we would hide nearby to watch the show.

The pilferers had seen the corn and ambled over. As they put their long grasping tongue around the ear, the electric shock hit them. They had lurched back, their tails in the air, stunned, and stared longingly at the corn. Unwilling to give up, they would attempt a heist. Again, the same shock! They had backed up, run and then, at a safe distance stood longingly staring at the corn. We had many laughs at the expense of the cows, and the corn was safe to continue ripening for the harvest.

Today as we rounded the next turn, the walnut trees still stood welcoming us with their majestic presence. They had provided shade for countless picnics and gatherings over the years.

I rushed to the nearby creek to view the trickling falls where my siblings and I had played as children. We had floated leaves in the water and raced them, tumbling over descending levels of rock shelves in the stream.

Brook Falls Creek, our playground

We had also gathered algae from the creek pools and called it snake poison. Alas! The creek had run dry; no splashing, tumbling water now. The falls, too, no longer flow like their storied past.

The curious new owner of this property suddenly appeared in his pickup truck just down the hill from his home. He asked who we were. After introductions, I attempted to share some of my memories of the farm. He was very cordial, tried to focus on my story, and then excitedly shared that his wife had just given birth so he was "a bit" distracted, but he did add that he liked the walnut trees, and he planned to keep them. Offering our congratulations on his new fatherhood, we all walked away, realizing yet another new generation was emerging. This property was no longer all I remembered, but it still held its special place for me, for my grandchildren, and the new father and young owner.

Even as I treasured the happy moments of the past, I was deeply bothered by the landscape before me. I silently followed my family back to the car. A worrisome thought hit me. Will the memories I shared today with them vanish like the past I described? There are no streets named after my parents; no memorial placards. For all appearances, it is as though they had never lived here.

Sadly, this was the end of the walk. I turned to my grandkids and said, "My parents' vision for us extends beyond signs and street names. We were so fortunate. They gave us values that helped shape our lives. As you grow older, like me, you will nurture and live by the values your parents have instilled in you." They laughed at my reference to being old.

Looking back at the landscape again, I wondered how I could recreate my life growing up here on these acres. As we departed, I felt an urgency to tell my story of how these roots on the farm shaped my odyssey. It was here I flew kites and dreamed of what could be.

The Raphael and Gerene Freiburger Farm   *circa 1960*

CHAPTER 2

Our Family Farm

1937 was a newsworthy year. Franklin Roosevelt was inaugurated for his second term, Adolph Hitler was the Chancellor of Germany, the Hindenburg exploded, the Mississippi River flooded its banks, the Golden Gate Bridge was opened, Amelia Earhart was lost in flight, and JRR Tolkien's *"The Hobbit"* was published. In the midst of all these banner headlines, I entered a quiet, nurturing world on April 1 as the first born on our family farm in Dubuque, Iowa.

Our farm was an animal nursery. Growing up, I picked up and admired fuzzy new baby chicks, pigs, and kittens. I searched for baby wild rabbits and marveled how a scrawny-looking baby robin came from a beautiful aqua egg. In the late summer I could sneak off and pluck a bright red apple or yellow pear off the tree. Frequently, I was sent to Mom's garden to gather pickles, cantaloupes, watermelons, carrots, tomatoes, grapes, corn, squash, potatoes, dill or eggplants for dinner.

In the fall and winter my life was full of caring for cows, dogs, cats, horses (ponies) and chickens. At every meal I drank fresh milk from the cows and ate healthy dinners of chicken, pork, and beef. And there was nothing like a fresh, delicious egg for breakfast. It was my world and I loved it. Every morning as I walked through the grass wet with dew to awaken the cows lying down in the pasture, another day of adventure on the farm began.

Each morning Dad opened the day—usually at 6 A.M. Dressed in his shirt and overalls, he stood in front of the picture of the Sacred Heart to say his prayers. He believed God took care of his family, the crops on the farm, and all the animals. He prayed that everyone in the family would have a good day.

When I heard him walk away after prayers, I knew I had to crawl out from under the covers. Almost always still feeling sleepy, I tried to hide, crawling way down to the foot of the bed under the blankets. My father found me although I thought I was totally tucked away. It was a game; I can still hear him chuckling to himself as he tried to uncover me.

A man of faith, Dad not only prayed for good crops, but he nurtured the soil as a gift from God. He was one of the first in the area to practice soil conservation. In the early 1950s, he asked the US Department of Agriculture Soil Conservation Service to design a plan for the

Image of the Sacred Heart posted on our kitchen wall

farm. The first step entailed strip cropping, a practice eliminating soil erosion into the waterways ultimately draining into the Mississippi River. Dad was preventing his topsoil from entering the flow of the river and being dumped into the Gulf of Mexico.

He was a pioneer in his day as an organic farmer and practiced what we today call "sustainability." When he won awards for these conservation practices, the local soil conservation officer would call Dad his "best customer and salesperson." I always saw Dad as that special person.

Dad was also an excellent tiller of the soil and entered many plowing contests. To plant the crops, he plowed the soil; the grass and other plants growing on the ground were covered under the topsoil. One day, Dad saw a notice about a local plowing contest in the *Farm Bureau Spokesman*. I went with him to meet the John Deere dealer. Dad asked the dealer to sponsor him, hoping to become the best plow operator in the state. The contest emphasized how well the furrows curled, covering the plants, and how evenly the plow entered the soil and exited at the ends of the plow field. Dad won the first contest and set out to win at the regional level!

[Photo at right] *"R.J. Freiburger was honored last week by the Dubuque Soil Conservation District for his many years of conservation farming. Freiburger who lives in Asbury has been a cooperator since 1950."*

The Telegraph Herald

© Karl Durkstein

Dad plowing – 1951, John Deere model 50

As a young admirer of my father's skill, I considered myself a partner accompanying him to these contests. I stood among the bystanders, stretching my neck to view the plowing contestants, wagging my finger and yelling, "That's my father plowing with the John Deere." When he won local, regional or state awards, I would sneak through the crowd to stand beside him during his interviews with radio or newspaper reporters. His soil conservation practices led to a celebrity role. Fred Wise, the photographer for John Deere tractor manufacturer publications, chose our farm to photograph hundreds of pictures. The farm, a model of soil conservation practices, also became a popular site for photographing new farm equipment. Soon pictures of Dad driving equipment around our contour strips were on calendars and in brochures advertising John Deere products all over the country. When one of my friends informed me how important his father was, I told him "Your father may be a big shot, but my father's picture is on calendars all over the world." Dad was my hero! But heroes are sometimes only pictures on calendars and live in a different world than their admirers. Yes, each time as a starry-eyed kid I looked up at that calendar, I wondered if I'd be as famous as my father when I grew up.

CHAPTER 3

Healing Our Bumps and Bruises

We had a sixth sense for each other's welfare as a tight-knit family. Although the machines on the farm had many moving parts, and although I was young and careless, I was fortunate not to experience any serious accidents. When I did suffer a cut or wound, I had the best nurse to care for me. My mother was a registered nurse, an unusual achievement for a woman in our community. Even before I had siblings, I kept her busy as a healer of my bumps, bruises, and illnesses.

A whole set of home remedies and medicinal concoctions from the Raleigh and Watkins men were part of my mother's healing process. The Raleigh truck arrived early in the month. The driver brought in his tray of salves, liniments and one-pill-cures-all.

Dad was always suspicious because the Raleigh guy arrived when he was working away from the house. Laughing as his truck approached one day while we were working in the field, he told me, "I think he has a case on your mother."

The real Raleigh winner was Camphor balm. My nostrils still burn when I think of that bottle. When I rubbed the camphor balm on a sore spot, I would turn my nose to avoid the acrid smell and I'd scrunch my eyes when nerve endings tingled.

Raleigh and Watkins products we used

The Watkins dealer arrived later in the month. We bought his remedies for our cuts and coughs. Dad purchased other concoctions for the animals. Using the Watkins salve was said to draw the infection right out of the wound. When applied, the skin turned a pallid white, and yes, the diseased area healed quickly. These traveling vendors' monthly visits replenished our supplies. I spent many nights before going to bed putting the salve on splinters, skinned shins, and cuts on my arms and legs.

Poultices and Epsom salts baths were the other home remedies. Most bandages were made of torn strips of shirts or other available cloths. Mom would split the end three-four inches, so that she could tie the bandage in place. The cut or bruise was carefully wrapped (as with an ACE bandage), and the "torn ends" were tied together. Often the bandages came untied, leaving a trailing stretch of cloth. I tried to rewrap it, but I was never able to make it look like Mom's professional bandaging.

While many families used castor oil with great frequency, my mother only associated its use with constipation. BAND-AIDS were just making their appearance. They were mostly applied at bedtime because they came loose during the day while I was working.

I had no awareness about bacteria and viruses. Most of the time, I simply wiped my hands clean. I did wash before meals! Only broken bones or stitches were tended to by the doctor. Mom had a special touch for handling everything else quite competently. Cuts, scrapes and black eyes were treated but not considered serious. Other kids in the neighborhood got away with pretending to be sick and stayed home from school. If I faked a temperature, Mom not only took my temperature but also punished me for lying. One time I faked it, and she made me hoe in the garden as punishment. I found out it's not easier to be sick than to have to hoe the garden.

Colds, impetigo, measles, mumps, and other diseases I caught in school challenged Mom and her remedies. She confined me to the house or made me stay in bed when I had these ailments. During my impetigo siege, highly contagious sores on the face, she reluctantly swabbed the sores with gentian violet. Sometimes even she didn't have the right cure for my ailments caught at school.

CHAPTER 4

The Collective Farm

My youthful world was built around living on a farm and attending our local church. The farm existed within a fenced boundary. My family ran its own business. We had our own animals, raised our own crops, and had our own religious life. Living in a cocoon, I wasn't aware at the time of a yearning to search for something beyond those boundaries.

I was content with the meaning of life learned in the Catholic Church we attended. Its teachings and rituals shaped our daily lives. Every morning I said my prayers. I prayed before and after meals. At night, I knelt by my bed to thank God for another day. I still see my father marking the Ember Days on the calendar. These were days set aside by our Church to pray, fast and thank God for the gifts of nature. When converting non-Christian nations, the Church had always tried to incorporate practices that led to good purpose. The Ember Days are an example. They occur at the beginning of the seasons ordered by the Church as days of fasting and abstinence. They were originally introduced to encourage fasting and praying, to thank God for the gifts of nature, to teach men moderation, and to assist the needy. Observance of the Ember days was my initiation into rituals.

Dad used the Ember Days as his guide. A good part of farming entailed predicting planting and harvest times, both dependent on weather patterns and seasonal changes such as the first frost. He penciled them in as marks on the calendar; they left a lasting impression on me. While watching my father I began to wonder if I would have a calendar to etch my future.

I remember as a young boy gathering little bags of our seeds to take to Church for a blessing on the Rogation Days each spring. In the Church's calendar, the four Rogation days are traditionally set apart for solemn processions to invoke God's mercy. The liturgical observance was the blessing of the seeds. This blessing instilled in me how dependent we were on God for a bountiful harvest and good things in our lives. I was further reminded by the blessings of the seeds that tiny things like seeds could evolve into greater things.

In our family, we placed great faith and trust in God as a provider. On the Rogation Days, we used to pray for rain. We used to select the seed carefully and express our faith that it would produce a better crop. Faith and trust depend on unknowns. In our family, we lived by religious rituals, a force binding everything together, giving it meaning and application. These practices became a core in my life. Even today when I plant garden seeds, I think back to seeds and their blessing on the farm.

My mother was a very devout Catholic, and she was one of the women who cleaned the church. She always talked about how special it was when Father Long came over to the church and visited while they were cleaning. When I watched the altar boys at Mass in their black cassocks and white surplices, I thought being an altar boy would be a way to have my own visits with Father Long.

When I reached 10 years old, studying to be an altar boy was special. I memorized Latin responses like "Ad Deum qui laetificat juventutum meum." (To God who gives joy to my youth) and learned all the proper rituals: when to ring the bell at the Consecration during Mass; when to move the missal at the altar, and how to assist at Communion. I was considered one of the best servers, so couples marrying in the parish often requested that I be one of the altar boys at their weddings. I liked doing this because couples usually gave me $2.00, sometimes $5.00. That was better than the $1.00 and the needles I got for cutting thistles for the neighbor.

I grew to understand rituals and while witnessing major milestones in peoples' lives, I began to appreciate these traditions.

My family and I gathered in our local parish church to celebrate Mass on Sundays and special feasts like Christmas and Easter. Father Long understood ritual and celebration. His sermons were plain spoken, and he talked about life and work on the farm. For our pastor, Church was a celebration of events. Every year he directed a Christmas play with parishioners playing different roles. One year my sister Margaret recited "'Twas the Night Before Christmas." I sang Christmas Carols as part of a teenage chorale. Older sisters would dress as angels and lead their brothers and sisters to the altar to receive their First Communion. Older brothers who weren't altar boys served as ushers and escorted their parents to the reserved seats where they were to sit.

Confirmation was another important event. Father Long encouraged each family to make it a coming of age celebration when their child turned 12. The Bishop who presided asked questions and each of the candidates eagerly raised a hand to answer. I got my chance and answered that I wanted to be confirmed and become a "soldier of Christ." During the ceremony, the Bishop anointed my forehead and then gave a gentle tap to my cheek, symbolic of becoming a "soldier of Christ." The older kids had told me my relatives were coming to see if I could endure the blow the Bishop would deliver. I was relieved to receive his gentle tap.

Christmas Eve Mass was Father Long's specialty. I stood in awe in the darkened sacristy as he would begin with his newly installed set of light switches. The strains of *"Silent Night"* would fill the church as the first soft light filtered into the nave. The pageantry would continue verse by verse, switch by switch until the spotlight illuminated the nativity scene nestled within the ten tall balsam trees. Everyone in church would ooh and aah as though they were the shepherds who had found Jesus. And then Mass would begin, and incense filled the air. I would feel totally uplifted. On these Christmas nights I wanted to be like Father Long. He always greeted parishioners with birthday wishes; he loved joining conversations in front of the church after Mass. He was genuinely devoted to the sick and dying, and an elegant ambassador of all things good in the Church.

My job as an altar boy was to make the charcoal glow so we could get an abundance of smoke. I took personal pride in this task. It was fun because I could create fire and smoke at church, and it was forbidden at home. I would light the charcoal chip and blow on it until the outside was white and the center glowed. I knew when the priest spooned on the incense it would make a billowing cloud of smoke. I took pride in making this happen. I became known as the incense maker among the altar boys, especially the younger ones who asked me to show them my secret to making the charcoal glow.

The Church was the center of my world. Father Long was a

frequent guest at our house. He came at planting time and harvest time. Each summer as we harvested oats, he would come for a noon time lunch. When I was 11 years old at one of those lunches, I excused myself and went over to listen to that day's bible story. In the background I heard Father Long tell my parents, "Jimmy is one of my best altar boys. I think he has a vocation to the priesthood." Pretending I didn't hear, I tried to focus on the bible story, feeling pretty good about myself.

Under the tutelage of its minister in our parish, we were cared for spiritually and guided toward our destinies. The Church provided real direction for my parents in "God's Little Acre," our farm. At the harvest, Dad would select the best yielding oats and save it as seed for the next crop. Utilizing his intuitive understanding of life (today we refer to it as DNA), he carefully chose new seeds and animals for breeding to improve each generation. Dad often said, "I want to leave this farm in better shape than I found it." Those words of my father were an insight for me. Slowly I realized that the same approach Dad took to nurturing his plants from generation to generation, resembled his inherent parenting style, driving me to improve my life.

CHAPTER 5

Moving Day

My parents moved three times during their married lives. The customary moving day was March 15, often accompanied by melting snow and mud. When I was a baby, Dad decided to farm and leave his day job. They moved a cow and a team of horses from Uncle Will's in Sageville to the Craig farm in Julien ten miles away. I remember Dad stopping at Mrs. Craig's big fancy house, walking up a set of steps, knocking on the door and handing her the rent money. She opened the door enough to take the money, said a quick thank you, and immediately shut the door. I couldn't believe, even though she lived in a nice house, that she didn't talk to him. I was four years old when we moved again; the Craig farm my parents were renting had been sold. I don't remember much about those early moves.

Our two-year stay at the Wernimont farm was difficult. The owner kept stopping by and telling Dad how to do his work. Finally, Dad had enough and said he didn't need anyone else to tell him how he should plant his crops. I agreed. My Dad knew how to farm.

The local pastor, Father Dunn, was the Mercy Hospital chaplain and knew Mom when she was in Nurses' training. When he heard that the First National Bank was selling a farm, he went to the bank president, Will Lawther, and told him he knew my parents and that he should sell the farm to them. Father Dunn later informed me he had told Lawther, "If you ever want to do one good thing in your life, you will sell the farm to the Freiburgers." That is how Dad and Mom made the purchase, paying $16,000, the bank holding the mortgage, for what would become the Freiburger homestead for the next 60 years. I was now five years old and finally old enough to help with this third and final move.

Moving day on the farm was like a circus. Chickens were crated, pigs gathered and loaded on a truck, and cows and horses herded from the present farm to the new location. We transported oats, corn, and hay to the new site for the animals. At the same time, we still had to pack, load, and move the house appliances and furniture. Moving became a special adventure for me as I tried to be part of the circus. helping crate chickens and load pigs. While neighbors bagged the oats, I held the sacks.

The most exciting event of the move was when our good friend Martin Jungk's truck got stuck in the mud with a load of crated chickens. Dad came to his and the chickens' rescue with the tractor. I hooked up the chain to the truck's bumper and stood on the tractor when dad pulled the truck out. What a sight. The chickens were cackling their 'Rescue us" as we pulled them out of the mud. I was so proud when Mr. Jungk asked if I would like to ride to the new farm with him.

Uncle Milton, who had a bigger truck, made about 20 round trips in the three mile stretch between the two farms. After loading his truck with animals or household goods, he asked me to keep him company on several of those rides. He made me feel extra special when he asked me to be his guide as he backed up the truck.

Family friends, Pete and Henry, loaded the truck; my Uncle Merle and Uncle Eldon helped unload at the new farm. On the final trip, I remember walking with a stick behind our herd of 15 cows along the road to the new farm. The county had just graded the road the season before. Roads were graveled, not paved as today. Gravel stones filled the middle part of the road, but the edges along the graveled area were sticky, wet clay. While walking behind the cows in that muck, my boots collected so much mud that I had a hard time walking. Finally, after eight hours of hauling, we unloaded the last truck load and we finally could say "We're home."

As darkness set in, we fed and milked the cows. There were chickens to be uncrated and fed in the hen house and pigs who needed settling in their new house and pen. After all the outdoor chores were completed, we faced a house filled with boxes and furniture.

Rose Arendt, Lizzie Jecklin, and Aunts Marie and Dorothy helped Mom unpack dishes and kitchen utensils. Uncles Norbert and Charlie attached stove pipes from the wood stove to the chimney, so Mom would be able to cook. Bill Ahrendt brought ice for the ice box. We didn't have electricity on the new farm. They had to unpack kerosene lamps to light the rooms and set up a kerosene heater to warm the house.

Finally, around 7 P.M. Aunt Dolores arrived with dinner. More than 15 relatives and friends stopped and enjoyed mashed potatoes and fried chicken. The room was filled with weary voices as we all enjoyed the feast, topped off by apple pie.

After dinner, I joined my brothers Tom, age four, and Don, age three, and crawled under the warm covers for a good night's sleep in our new upstairs bedroom. The move was over and in my five-year-old mind, I felt like an important helper in this major event.

I was happy to join 25 new faces in the one room Asbury school. From now on I would proudly walk a new road to school with a set of kids my age. I could now tell them my parents owned their own farm.

CHAPTER 6

The Wonder of Life

New life was popping up all over each spring. After the brooder house heater was warmed, Mom and I held each fuzzy yellow peeping baby chick, freshly arrived from the hatchery, and placed it under the warm heater. Little piglets came from their mother's womb and nestled to suckle their first milk under the warmth of the heat lamp hovering overhead. Calves would struggle to stand for the first time after a total grooming by their mother's tongue. The pets, too, continued their lineage. Newly emerged kittens, still unable to see, struggled to stay warm near their mother. Puppies, still a bit too weak to walk, snuggled in the warmth of their mother's breasts. I spent my day mystified by the colored markings on the kittens and the black, white and yellow spots and stripes on the puppies. I marveled as the yellow fuzz of the baby chicks became long white feathers.

And the blooming plants welcomed spring. I wandered around the yard, pulling dandelions, rubbing their yellow coloring on my cheeks. The crocuses were too fragile to pick, so I just knelt and blew them to watch them shimmer. Choosing the largest daffodil bloom, I picked it to give to Mom. The favorite shrub of all was Mom's yellow rose bush. I watched in awe as one rose bud would appear, and then suddenly the whole bush would be adorned with petite yellow roses. I avoided the thorns when I picked the first bouquet for the kitchen table.

In awe I watched the bees enter apple tree blossoms and come out with a coating of yellow pollen. I was puzzled when Mom told me that the bees and flowers were like parents of the bright red apples that came later in the year. And other crops added their chapters to a new generation. We carefully planted the oats, corn, and alfalfa seeds of the past year for a new yield. It always struck me that we had to do so much work for the crops in the fields, while at the same time the new life of animals seemed to happen while we watched. I was filled with a sense of wonder, seeing new life bursting all around me.

On a Good Friday morning when I was eight, my Mom taught me the facts of potato life. "Go fetch some buckets, Jimmy. We're going to plant potatoes." She began moving and sorting potatoes in the large bin where they were stored. "Mom, we eat potatoes from that bin! Don't we need to use potato seeds to grow potatoes?" She called me over and said, "I'll show you what I am looking for."

She held up a potato and there was a little plant like structure growing on the skin of the potato. I took the potato to look at it, "That potato feels rotten." Then she said, "We only think about one part of a potato's life—eating it as food. But the actual spud we eat is a source of energy for a new potato to grow. Under the peel is a very starchy, rich food."

She held up another potato and pointed out little dark spots that look like warts, "eyes," she called them and told me this story. "When the potato lives in a warm, dry or moist area, little sprouts grow from these eyes. I'm looking for potatoes that have those sprouts. Do you see the three sprouts on the potato you are holding in your hand? I'll cut the potato into pieces; each piece will have a sprout on it."

"Good, I sure wouldn't want to eat this potato. But I'm glad we can use it as a seed." Mom looked at me quizzically and said, "Jimmy, it's not a seed. Seeds are in apples, oranges, blackberries, and other fruits. This potato is a tuber. Tubers are types of specially enlarged plant structures filled with lots of nutrients. Plants use them to survive the winter or dry months. The tubers provide nutrients during the growing season." She continued, "That's why they are a good food: They are rich in carbohydrates and vitamins, sources of energy for us. And the wonderful thing is we can eat them as mashed, baked and even as potato chips." I still wasn't sure about tubers, but I agreed about how we ate potatoes.

After my mother had cut the potatoes into pieces, each having an eye, I took a bucket full of the pieces, went out to the field, and placed them in the ground, "two shoes" apart. I stood in the furrow, a long, five-inch-deep ditch my father had made with his plow. Then I placed the heel of my left foot by the potato piece and the heel of my right foot at the toe of the left—so that made the distance "two shoes." We then took a hoe and covered the potato pieces. Each piece by the end of the summer would multiply into 5-8 tubers. We dug these tubers with a fork that had several steel tongs, much larger than the forks we used to eat our food.

I often walked out to the field where we had planted the potatoes to check if they were growing. At first there were tiny little plants with broad leaves. Then they grew almost as tall as my knees. I ran home one day to ask Mom, "Why do the potatoes have flowers? Are they growing seeds?" She thought for a moment, "No, remember potatoes have tubers, not seeds. The flowers are a sign that the tubers were beginning to form. In a couple of weeks, we can dig little potatoes, tubers, the size of a golf ball."

The potato story introduced me to the wonder of plants dying and growing again each season. As summer came, I observed all the plants I could find to see if they had seeds. When I ate an apple, I asked my mother if the part we ate was food for the seeds in the core. Then I began to explore oranges, cucumbers, and, oh yes, corn. We also had watermelon on the fourth of July—wow, talk about seeds and food for seeds to grow! Suddenly, it dawned on me that we had wonderful food all summer because the plants had produced seeds for the next year's growth. Looking at all the plants growing in Mom's garden, I tried to imagine how many plants the seeds from one cucumber or watermelon would produce. Then I walked away and said to myself, "That's why Mom can give everyone who comes, something from the garden. She has a lot of different kinds of seeds planted."

At Easter, my mother bought 50 little baby chicks. One day I was watching these tiny yellow creatures who had no feathers. While I was listening to their "peep, peeping," I asked my mother how chickens were born. She told me they hatched from eggs. Then I made another amazing discovery. My mother used to sell eggs. People came every week to buy them. We had eggs for breakfast, and my favorite school lunch was a fried egg sandwich.

But I was concerned. I asked, "Have I been eating little chickens when I eat eggs?" Mom said, "No, only eggs that are kept in a warm incubator for 21 days have baby chickens in them. It takes that long for the baby chicken to grow inside the egg. The eggs we eat are fresh and do not have baby chickens in them."

"Mom, do some chickens lay eggs that don't have little chickens in them? How do we know the difference? How do you tell?" All chickens look alike." She looked at me quizzically, then smiled, saying "No, Jim, it's not the chicken, it's the egg. The newly laid egg is held up to a bright light to see if there is a little chicken inside. Those eggs go to the incubator. We eat the others.

"In those eggs where the baby chicken is growing, the white and yellow parts are food. As the egg is food for you, it is also the food the baby chicken needs to eat 'to break out of its shell.' That is why eggs are such good food; they provide all the food a baby chicken needs for 21 days while it is growing inside the shell."

So, I now knew the chicken story, so I began to look around the farm at the other animals. There were grown up pigs and baby piglets every year. The same for the cows; even the cats had kittens. And then I began to think about plants, animals, and SEASONS! I got it! It happened every year.

But why are people different? We just seem to have birthdays every year. Everything, potatoes, chickens and seasons are new. How about us?

I asked Mom the puzzle about people. She explained to me that people plant and dig the potatoes; we feed and give the chickens a home. We do this for all the plants and animals. We are just smarter and different. That is why we are in charge. Remember, she explained, we wear different clothes each season. Animals don't change their clothes, and the plants can no longer live when the weather gets cold. Humans are different than plants and animals; we choose when we want to marry someone and have a family. Animals and plants can't do that.

At eight-years old, I was filled with amazement at all the life stories around me—new plants, old plants; baby chickens, old hens and roosters; plants growing in the spring, plants dying in the winter; baby animals born in the spring, then growing old and wearing feathers or warm coats in the winter. As one of the "people," I could decide what I needed to eat and what to wear to keep warm. People nurture and protect all these life events on our farm. I just thought it was wonderful to be a human being and wanted to grow up being a part of all these goings on.

This was the first wonder I experienced growing up on the farm. Over time there would be many others.

CHAPTER 7

Just Like Dad

Growing up on our small farm with its early risings, working with animals, and cultivating crops, created a special bond among my parents, siblings, and me. I never kept track of hours or how old I had to be to work. Farming is one occupation where child labor laws do not apply. Farm life is a twenty-four hour a day, seven-day-a-week occupation. Farmers deal with living things—cows need milking, animals need feeding, horses need grooming and harnessing, and crops require tending and harvesting on a timely basis. Even in the winter, chores are ever present.

In our work clothes; shirts and dresses made from feed sacks.
Left to right: Back row: Dad, Don, Margaret, Jim, Tom, Mom
Front row: Mike, Willie, and Mary Jo Circa 1952

My siblings and I had to find a place for school and visitors in our busy farm lives filled with chores, animals, the weather, and working in the fields. Each day I learned how to care for the animals and provide food for them and ourselves. My father taught me about rotating corn, oats, and alfalfa hay to enrich the soil and ensure food for the animals. Mom taught me uses for every shrub and tree on the farm.

I became an expert, regaling city visitors with how I helped Mom with the many foods we ate. I picked gooseberries to make pies. Blackberries (although the bushes had many thorns) were wonderful for dessert and jam; walnuts and butternuts were best in Christmas cookies; and elderberries were good for both wine and jam. I enjoyed picking morel mushrooms, helped Mom dry them, and use them for cooking. I experimented with other tastes, too. Before Dutch Elm disease destroyed so many trees, I would strip the inside lining of the bark, chew it like gum, and spit out the juice from the chomped lining as if it were tobacco. After a few slimy experiences, I decided I'd stick with morels.

My Dad named every animal and every tool had a special use and purpose. I had my own special shovel and my own favorite among the farm cats, Gertie. Often imagining to be grown up, I would sneak off and mount the idle tractor and pretend to drive it.

When I was ten, Dad decided I was old enough to pull the clutch handle and stamp on the brakes of our John Deere Model A. He took me for a test drive in the fields. I passed the test. Now I was a real operator. He let me handle the tractor by myself. The next day was special; he asked me to start the tractor and take a wagon to the field. I was nervous but felt proud. I told my brother Tom that driving the tractor was easy.

As his oldest son, my dad relied on me to help with planting and harvesting the crops. When he asked me, I always felt he was preparing me to follow in his footsteps. When we planted the oats, he drove the horses over the prepared field, and I shoveled the oats seeds into a spreader, swirling them over the earth below. After sowing the oats, we prepared the other fields for planting corn. Dad used to tell me that according to *The Farmer's Almanac*, the time to plant corn began, "when the oak tree leaves are the size of squirrels' ears."

Planting corn seeds, Dad rode on the planter seat and steered the horses across the long field. I dreamed of the day when I would sit in that seat and plant just like him. When he cultivated the corn, I rode on the back of the tractor. As we drove along, I uncovered any little corn stalks buried in dirt by the cultivator shovels.

Learning to drive the tractor was the first stage in my future mastery. I became a real big-time operator when Dad asked me to get on the tractor and cultivate. He told my younger siblings, Tom and Don, to ride on the back of the tractor like I had done when he cultivated. Although they preferred Dad's driving, riding with me meant they were on their way to becoming the next drivers. I tried to imitate my father, concentrating on guiding the tractor and the safety of the rider behind me. I wanted to be head of my own farm, just like Dad.

Chapter 8

Toys are Toys

Tom, Don, and I spent a lot of time designing and creating toys. Play-time boats, plows to prepare fields for seeds, and even pirouetting flying projectiles—we made them all. Usually we employed our creative energies in down time—no work in the fields, no fences to build before the evening chores. We built a whole collection.

My specialty was making bows and arrows. A willow branch, very pliable, was bent into the shape of a bow. I attached string to one end of the branch, put the string end on the ground, bent the limb in an arc and attached the string to the other end. The string was very taut, and my willow "bow" had real snap. The arrows were reeds that had dried over the winter. I placed the larger end of the reed at the center of the string, pulled back on the string—and I had a bow and arrow. With a thicker willow branch, the arrow could fly 100 feet.

We created more than hunting tools. Living on the farm, we directed our inventions toward farm work. Some of the groceries came in tin cans. Cutting a piece of tin can and then folding a corner, we made a plow. John Deere, who had invented the first steel plow, would have been envious of us. I think we invented the first tin plow.

Imitating Dad plowing and preparing the field, we would make our own furrows in the dirt with the tin plows, harrow the furrows with corn cobs, and using an imaginary corn or oats seeder to plant the crops. We spent a lot of time tilling soil on our own little acres, just the way Dad did.

When we were young, our soldiers fought in World War II. There was much talk about bombers and artillery. Tom, Don and I created our own artillery using corn cobs after the chickens had eaten the kernels on the ears of corn and gathered feathers shed by the chickens. The center of blunt end of cob was soft. We stuck the quill ends of two feathers in this section of the cob. We threw the feathered cobs as artillery with the smaller, pointy end aimed towards our target. When launched, the feathers would spin the cob and make it follow a course directly to the target area.

I did cheat a bit on our manufacturing of toys. *Kellogg's Corn Flakes* advertised a model B 24 bomber at a cost of two dollars and ten box tops. It had a bomb bay and mirror for dropping marble bombs. In the fall of 1942, I coerced my two brothers and sister into eating a lot of corn flakes.

At last I had my bomber. I would walk around the room, holding it up as if flying. Then I would open the bomb bay, use the mirror inside the bomb bay for sighting, and drop a marble on my target. It took a while before I finally figured out there was a reverse image in the mirror.

We did more than hunt and farm with our toys. We made boats and had races. We would take wood shingles and cut out a notch at one end. Reusing the piece of the shingle we had cut out, we would cut it in half, make a slit in one piece, and slide the pieces together, forming a propeller.

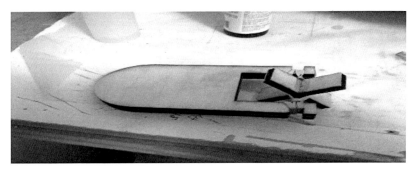

Toy Boats

Placing the propeller in the notch opening we had made in the original shingle, we would stretch either a piece of inner tube or a heavy rubber band around the edges of the shingle, creating a boat and propeller. The surface of the water tank where the cows and horses drank provided the racing arena.

To propel the boats, we would wind the propeller until the rubber band was tightly stretched. In most races, the boats traveled alongside each other. Often the propeller would spin out before we could get it into the water. Sometimes the boat would turn and go in the opposite direction. We had to schedule races before or after the animals drank to be sure they didn't disrupt our races.

In the evenings when we had visitors, the house lawn became our playground. The more common games were *Statue, Captain May I,* and *Red Rover.* Frequently, the lawn behind the house served as a croquet court.

As we got a bit older, the adults invited us to play card games. The most popular were *euchre* and *500.* We kids played as partners and opposed Dad and Leslie. Leslie, who monthly tested the milk produced by our cows, was good at cheating in card games. We finally caught on one night when he played the joker twice. We did a lot of shouting and laughing during these games.

One of our playtime ventures had a serious outcome. Don and Margaret were playing together in the big bedroom in the house where Dad had stored in the closet, the seed corn for planting. Don and Margaret made "birthday cakes," spreading peanut butter on graham crackers, with kernels of seed corn as decorations. The seed corn had been coated with mercury to prevent it from rotting in the bag.

Margaret became very ill, went into convulsions and was taken to the hospital with mercury poisoning. Mom sat with her, praying that she would not die. After two days Margaret came out of the convulsions and recovered. Everyone in the family spent much of those two days praying that she would survive. After that scare, we were very careful in choosing our play items.

In my younger years, I had played many games taking me very close to the edge. Thankfully I survived, but I sometimes look at scars on my shin or my crooked index finger and see the evidence of the price I paid for some of those games.

CHAPTER 9

My Future as a Farmer

Driving the tractor was one of the fun jobs for me while the hardest and dirtiest job on the farm was making hay. The days were hot, and dust was everywhere. We had to wear long-sleeved shirts and pants to protect ourselves from the itchy hay dust. Perspiration from the long hours under the sun drenched my whole body.

As the oldest son, I did all four steps at one time or another in making hay. Sitting behind a team of horses on the mower, I cut the hay. When it dried, I drove the horses and raked it into rows called windrows. Being a tall and gangly ten-year old, I graduated into "bucking the loader," loading the hay on the wagon lifted by the loader from the ground.

We then removed hay from the wagon at the barn using a large grapple fork. My role was to "stick the fork," pushing the tongs of the fork into the hay on the wagon. The fork was attached to a long rope that pulled the load into the barn. My brother Don led one of the horses hitched to the other end of the rope which pulled the fork load of hay into the hayloft. We repeated this cycle, usually about ten times, until the wagon was unloaded.

After five unloadings during the afternoon and with three more still waiting for me, I would be relieved to see my six-year old sister Margaret's coming down the path with lemonade and cookies. Oh, did they taste great! Those refreshing treats spurred me on to finish those last three loads of the day.

After completing the transfer of the hay around 5 P.M., we unhitched the horses and set them free. The horses, too, had had a long day and moved slowly. They immediately went to the water tank and consumed gallons.

At last I could take off my dusty, itchy, sweaty clothes. We didn't have indoor plumbing for showering or an outdoor swimming area. We sought relief by sitting under the pump soaping, soaking, and washing ourselves.

On quieter summer days we built fences. Dad measured the distance between posts by walking heel to toe, ten times. Then I would brag to him, "Watch how fast I'll dig those fence post holes." Digging through the soft earth with a shovel, every ten minutes I would burrow down two feet, making a hole large enough for the oak posts. When the fence line was long, I imagined myself a woodchuck, sometimes digging 50 holes. Often looking back at the piles of dirt around the holes, I sheepishly made a fist to see if wood chucking would permanently cramp my hands.

We placed the posts in the holes. Dad had a wooden tamper that he claimed, "dated back 20 years first used by his father." As I filled the hole, he pounded his tamper, most of the time on the dirt in the hole. After the dirt was piled high around the post, he'd stomp the ground with his shoes and shake the post, claiming this added life to the post. I used to chuckle to myself about Dad's magic shoes.

Totally immersed in life on the farm, my contact with the outside world came from the radio, the newspaper, and storyteller visitors who came to the farm to share their stories. Bill Ahrendt, whom I loved like a grandfather, told me about driving through the mountains. I'd never traveled far from our Iowa farm, and at seven years of age, I was fascinated that hills existed taller than the bluffs rising by the Mississippi River I knew so well. Some nights after those long days of haying, I would drift off to other kinds of work that didn't involve haying. I thought about being a mailman like Bill Ahrendt. He didn't have to make hay.

I didn't share my concerns about not being a farmer. As a ten year old I was still trying to follow in my father's footsteps and making hay was necessary. I loved the idea of farming when I thought about Dad's magic shoes and my Grandpa's tamping stick. But my little farm cocoon was becoming porous.

Chapter 10

Asbury ... My Hometown

For eighteen years I lived on a farm nestled among a network of farms surrounding a little town. It was named after Bishop Francis Asbury, a British-born Methodist, who had built a church and carried on missionary work as far west as Nebraska. Our pastor, Father Long, told us that although the town and road through this town were named after a Methodist bishop, most of the people who lived here in 1949 attended our church, St. Philomena.

The town center boasted a grocery store, tavern, and hall owned by the Horton family. A dozen houses and a one-room elementary school lined the sides of Asbury Road with the two churches, Catholic and Methodist, serving as bookends.

The Horton Store stocked most of our family's needs. We picked up the Sunday paper after Mass and bought our food staples there. I remember the store for its candy and gum. We nicknamed the woman who ran the store *"Tiny"* Horton because we could hardly see her behind the counter.

The bar in the same building, *"Horton's Tavern,"* opened at noon during the week and was usually busier than the store. Tiny's husband, Jim, bartended. Occasionally, my Dad, with me in tow, stopped by to have a beer and catch up on the local news. I liked these visits because even as a little guy, I could sit on the stool and drink a coke while listening to the men talk.

The hall adjoining the store was the community meeting place and the home of raucous euchre card game tournaments. The hall was always crowded if a town meeting was called. That same hall hosted wedding receptions, and I attended my first one there. I was captivated by the two musicians, one of whom played an accordion while the other sang. On another occasion, we joined our neighbor Lizzie to celebrate her birthday with a roasted pig and tubs filled with bottled beer.

Asbury's county road grader with its cab, extended frame, and angled road blade was parked next to the Horton Hall and was considered a town monument. The road grader gained a new neighbor in the 1950s. The town erected a volunteer fire department building near the Horton Store and several men in the community acted as volunteer firefighters. The Horton Store would receive calls about the fire and sound the town fire siren alert. The volunteers drove with sirens screeching and lights flashing to the fire truck garage. After donning their fire gear, they raced to the fire site in the engine accompanied by a flotilla of trucks and cars with sirens screaming. If we heard the sirens, Dad and I would follow the flotilla to the fire site to see if we could assist. I recall feeling scared and sad seeing one of our neighbor's buildings on fire. It was a whole different experience when Dad and I piled and burned brush. Then I was fascinated by those fires' crackles and sparks.

It was fun to visit the shiny red and silver fire truck. When no one was looking, I would climb into the driver's seat and pretend I was heading to a fire, saving my neighbor's home. On one of those pretend drives, I realized not everything can be saved. The firefighters sometimes saw houses and barns of their neighbors destroyed.

One of their first calls to action summoned the firefighters to Mike Batton's house on fire. Although they couldn't save the house, they extinguished the fire and saved the rest of the farm buildings. After the fire, my father and a couple of neighbors summoned others to help cut logs and saw them into lumber. Other neighbors poured cement for the foundation of the Batton's new house. Working together, they built a new structure on the burned-out site.

The Batton family moved into their new dwelling a few weeks after the fire. My family and other neighbors held a welcoming party for the Battons in their new home. I went from room to room with Michael Batton, my third-grade classmate, looking at the furniture, bedding, and clothing neighbors had donated. Each family had also prepared a specialty dish for a sumptuous dinner, and we all celebrated late into the evening.

I couldn't believe that all ten neighbors had built a new home in one month and gathered for the celebration. Each farm may have had a fenced boundary, its own breed of cows, and individual brand of machinery, but the whole community shared the Batton family's happiness with their new home.

The Lewis family, original owners of my family's farm, had traded a strip of land with Jacob Batton to gain entry from the main road to their farm. We called this narrow stretch of land, our lane. It was a private road, and we had the responsibility of grading, graveling, fencing and snow removal in winter.

Garden and lane to the main road

Dad hired Emil Nebel, the road grader operator, to clean up the ditches and level the lane each spring. Dad had worked out an arrangement with him to grade our lane. Emil maintained the gravel roads and plowed the snow. He gave Emil a fifth of whiskey to clear the ditches and level the roadbed. Emil considered it part of his route. He would make a big looping turn going down our lane to the buildings, rev the engine when he saw us kids gawking by the barn, and then turn back towards the main road.

In winter, the lane attracted windswept snow like iron gathers on a magnet. I remember praying it wouldn't snow because even a few flakes meant getting out the shovels. When we shoveled, we moved the snow to the edges, forming two banks. Each storm would result in snow filling the space between the banks. I grew weary of these repeated shovelings.

When I was ten years old, we had an exceptionally heavy snow storm. The drifts were so deep it took a week for the county to plow the snow on the main roads. It also took us a week to shovel through the four-to-five-foot drifts in our lane. During that week, the eggs and cream accumulated because no one could drive the road to reach the farm. Dad had to find a way to deliver them. He hitched the horses to the wagon, handed me a blanket, and asked me to come along as we hauled cream to a dairy and eggs to Brammers Grocery in Dubuque. Along the way many people came out and waved to us calling Dad by name. I told him that it felt like we were in a parade and all these people recognized him from the calendar pictures. They all had come out to cheer him as a famous person. He chuckled. He could care less about being famous. He just wanted to get the eggs and milk delivered.

CHAPTER 11

The Center of My Life—My Parents

My father sat in the sunroom in his rocking chair after lunch, which we called dinner. He listened to the weather report, the stock market report on grain and pork bellies, and the Paul Harvey news broadcast. In her own chair in the same room, Mom would go through the bills, read or crochet. They also talked, and during that time, my siblings and I would play on the lawn, usually dreading the afternoon's chores. My parents used this time together to plan because the evenings were spent visiting others, hosting visitors, or going to bed early.

As a family, we had a great variety of visitors on the farm. My father was a storyteller. He enjoyed farm visitors and entertained them. My mother was the local source of fresh produce. I don't remember anyone leaving without eggs or vegetables from the garden.

Many relatives and people from different walks of life and areas of the state and county came frequently. Everyone had a story, too. We had so many visitors, it seemed like a boarding house at times. I remember waking up in the middle of the night to discover Uncle Marv and Aunt Erma sleep-

My father in his favorite chair catching up on the latest changes in farm practices.

ing in my brothers' and my bedroom. I had gone to bed before they arrived and was totally startled by their presence when I woke up. I quietly got up and tiptoed out of the room hoping not to wake them.

In those days, the vendors and barbers came to the farm. One frequenter was my father's cousin, Gus, who had a barbershop in Dubuque. Gus would come, put the barber cloth on us, and cut our hair in the kitchen. The total bill for my father, me, and my two brothers, Tom and Don, was a chicken dinner. The cost of each haircut was a bottle of beer. I always wanted to go first; the last haircut was the casualty of several bottles of beer.

Gus was a great storyteller and lover of Ford cars. With each new question about his car and another bottle of beer, his Ford would go ten mph faster. My brothers and I once contrived a plan to deal with his Ford braggadocio. We jacked up the car and put it on four wooden blocks, leaving the tires an inch above the ground. After several beers and haircuts, we challenged him to show us what his Ford could do. A bit juiced, he got in the car, started it up, put it in reverse and revved the motor. Nothing happened. He jumped out of the car, totally mystified and scratching his head. We were quite proud of our mischief, removed the blocks, had a good laugh, and sent him on his way.

Dad and Mom had a special talent for drawing people to come and visit our home. I learned from them the art of gathering people, listening to their ideas, opinions, stories, and making every visitor feel important.

Although great hosts, in the solitude of their relationship on the farm, my parents constantly bickered and showed little outward affection toward one another. Growing up I accepted their external lack of intimacy. As a thirteen-year old, I was totally startled while accompanying my father to visit Mom in the hospital when Dad went over and kissed her good night before we left. I had never seen him kiss or hug her.

I don't remember ever being hugged by my parents. They expressed their love for me by changing my diapers as a baby, picking me up and putting band aids on my scuffed knees, buying me combat boots for shoes, sending me to a private high school, checking my homework, and helping pay for college. They were always there for me. Mom was a stalwart for my education. Dad was there to teach me the farm chores and when I needed a ride to school or church. Those were their signs of love.

My Parents Wedding, January 14, 1936

My Siblings – 2018
Left to right: Back row: Mike, Me, Tom, Don, Willie
Front row: Margaret, Mary Jo

Chapter 12

My Father

My father was the fourth child in his family. While his older brother tended to domineer, his two older sisters nurtured him. He eventually became the go-between his older brother and the ten younger ones in the family. When his family needed a negotiator, they called Raphael. My dad grew up in a very culturally defined world. He told me, "I learned how to be a farmer from my father. The measure of a good farmer is the quantity of crops he harvests to maintain the quality of his livestock." My dad's whole life was dedicated to that cycle of life.

Dad saw his parenting role as preparing me to follow in his footsteps, as he had done with his father. His view of my success was the degree I would carry on the same tradition. It was important to be known as Raphael Freiburger's son, in my case, the eldest son who would continue his work, owning land and farming as he did. In my early years, I tried to imitate Dad's routine, waiting for him to tell me he would have done it that same way.

But as the oldest son, I discovered a larger world than the fields and animals of the farm. I was a voracious reader and as a youngster read books like Richard Halliburton's *The Book of Marvels*. I enjoyed reading books describing different cultures and wonders in the world. Sometimes I would sit and dream about visiting those places.

Dad's Role in the Neighborhood

Our friends and neighbors respected my father. I wanted to be like him. In our Asbury community, there were brothers who did not speak to each other. Even though our neighbors Mike and Ray squabbled, Dad could get along with each of them. When the Batton's house burned, it was my dad who rallied the community to rebuild their home.

The neighborhood parents asked Dad to be the adult leader when the 4-H club was founded. When he got involved in neighborhood quarrels, my mother got upset and strongly voiced her concern. Her sense of negotiating focused on what she thought was right, and most of the time, she found it hard to accept a middle ground.

At family gatherings, Dad was the first to join games, tell stories, or just be a good host. I always enjoyed his stories. When we had company, I was often captivated as he embellished yarns about his youth. In one story of his early years, he described making human dummies and putting them on the road. According to Dad, in those years the automobile headlights were not very bright. Drivers on country roads came along, ran over the dummy with a noticeable bump, and then stopped, thinking they had run over a person. Meanwhile, my father and his gang would pull the dummy off the road with a rope. When the driver came back to search for a body, it had disappeared. Dad would get up and walk around the room, imitating the frustrated husband looking for the body. Then he would mimic a "post-accident" attempt by the driver attempting to alleviate his wife's anxiety about running over someone. His description was so vivid I always had a vicarious experience of the incident.

From my earliest years I appreciated his stories. Only later in life would I appreciate my father's values. A man of integrity in every way, he pioneered new methods of farming long before they were fashionable.

He cultivated his land the way he guided his life. He taught me the value of honesty as I watched him check the scale so he would not charge a penny more than the weight of the sacks of oats a neighbor purchased. He developed friendships with neighbors based on trust. He never ran for a county or local office, but his support helped many win an election.

Dad valued everything comprising the farm: his crops, his animals, the buildings, and the machinery. He walked and inspected the entire 160 acres with his favorite dog, Sport. He beamed with pride when he showed me an ear of corn, fully kernelled, grown without artificial fertilizer. Each newly turned furrow was perfectly curled like the ones I had proudly seen him turn when he won plowing contests.

The Old Model A

No memory of my Dad is complete without including the 1930 Model A car. I associate so much of what we did in our family with him and that car. When I complained the rear window didn't work, Dad defended the car and told me to turn the handle right. Loyalty to the Model A ranked second only to the horses on our farm.

I can still hear the sound of the Model A horn. That horn was Dad's signature greeting to our neighbors. He scared the horses tooting and chasing them in the fields, and the horn announced his arrival to pick my siblings and me up after school. The Model A, a grand old car, rose approximately 18 inches from the ground and could plow through drifts of snow and never get stuck in the springtime muddy roads. When we drove the twenty miles to visit our grandparents in Buena Vista, we waved from the car as we passed by the unlucky people forced to walk because their cars had gotten stuck in the mud. The Model A was so dependable we could go anywhere. Its only failure was blowing a piston and needing a new motor.

Our Model A was a touring luxury. The manual shift was not synchronized with the clutch, so Dad would often grind the gears when backing up or starting forward. But when he got the car in third gear, we would go cruising along on our gravel roads at 45 miles an hour with the front windshield tilted open and the back windows rolled down halfway, creating a breeze through the car on hot days.

The cold winter months were another issue. Instead of a heater for the passengers, the Model A had makeshift cover over the manifold, directing heat into the car when the motor warmed up, but not enough to reach Tom, Don, Margaret, and me shivering in the backseat. Close to freezing on cold day drives, we bundled ourselves in blankets. During long trips the windows frosted over, and I specialized in drawing figures and writing on the glass. Without a car radio, we would sing, tell stories, or read.

One winter when the Model A sat for a couple of days before a North Buena Vista drive, mice found the cover over the manifold a convenient nesting place. Halfway through our drive, we all had to get out of the car and stand shivering by the roadside after the mice met their fate leaving behind their horrific stench. Dad finally found the nest and cleaned out the area. We still held our noses for the remainder of the trip trying to minimize the lingering putrid odor.

Model A Dashboard

The car had an interesting dashboard with a key area, a temperature gauge, a gas tank gauge, and a speedometer at the bottom that constantly shivered from left to right. The gas tank was housed in front of the windshield with the gas tank cap prominently displayed. The head lights attached to the fenders and radiator, faintly illuminated the road at night.

Two parking lights, attached to the hood of the car on the right and left of the windshield, added light for driving at night or in foggy conditions. The starter was on the floor between the clutch and the long shift lever. The horn, the spark lever, and the throttle were on the steering wheel.

When starting the car, Dad would adjust the spark lever and pulled down the throttle lever. He sometimes scared us when he deliberately pulled the spark lever down, creating a loud "backfire bang," shooting sparks out the tail pipe. When we would go grocery shopping, my parents had to load everything in the back seat because the Model A had no trunk. I rode many times alongside a case of our eggs on the way to the Brammer's Grocery. They traded the eggs for the groceries we needed to buy. On the way home, the newly purchased groceries were stacked high beside me.

We didn't have a refrigerator, so Dad bought 2 X 3-foot ice blocks for our ice box. He used an ice tongs to carry the ice and he put the blocks of ice on the back-seat floor. I always wanted Dad to buy the ice last because my legs had to endure leaning on the cold blocks for a shorter time on the way home. The shopping tour was completed when we went to the Sunbeam day-old bread stores to buy sandwich bread. Although Mom baked bread a couple of times a week, we still needed sandwich bread which was stashed on the ice for the ride home.

The Model A held a treasury of stories. It hauled potatoes, oats, chickens, groceries, and kids. Dad drove it to explore the farm's many nooks and crannies. Alas, we finally had to part company with that dear Model A. In 1950 Dad bought a blue Ford Fairlane with a sun visor. But the Model A had lived up to its reputation until the end.

When my father went to negotiate a loan for the purchase of the new Ford, he dealt with Will Lawther at the First National Bank. Lawther, an older man, said to Dad, "I can only give you $75 for the Model A." Dad was put off and with a dismissive tone said , "Why are you so cheap? It ran ten years for me and has a new motor."

The banker replied, "It's an old car and isn't worth much!" Dad fired back, "Neither are old men." Dad ultimately settled for the $75.

I thought about Dad and Will Lawther's conversation. Despite my father's defensive retort and initial urge to argue, I sensed he realized he had to say goodbye to his Model A. I observed his horizons widen. I realized I was seeing mine change, too.

Chapter 13

My Mother

My mother's family moved from the City of Dubuque to an isolated, rural setting when she was ten. She was the oldest girl; she had three brothers, one older and two younger, and two younger sisters. Her father was a much sought-after carpenter, his work taking him away from home much of the time. Her mother emerged as the dominant parent in the family. The result was favoritism among the children. As the oldest girl, Mom had a difficult relationship with her mother. Gramma Bauer strongly favored the two younger sisters over Mom. As the eldest daughter, my mother had a close relationship with her father. This created a quarrelsome relationship among the siblings.

At 12 years old, she left home and traveled by train to live with her grandparents in Monona to attend high school. Those four years greatly influenced her life. Although strict and traditional, her grandparents instilled a sense of ambition in my mother. Their influence led her to pursue a nursing degree. Upon completing nursing's training eight years after she left home, she was at the zenith of breaking through her family's lifestyle and creating a new life for herself. She specialized in surgical nursing and graduated from the program first in her class. Her life reflected that challenging role; although her insights were scalpel sharp, her personal comments to others sometimes made unnecessary incisions.

When she married my father,

My Mother, Gerene Bauer, graduated at top of her class.

she left a highly competitive, successful nursing career and became a housewife and mother, relegated to a male-dominated world, just like other women of her generation. Her timing and achievements did not serve her well.

I don't think my mother ever resolved this role shift. I remember Dad and her constantly in disagreement. In the 1930s, through the 1950s, the man was recognized as the head of the family, the one in charge. I remember when Vincent Batton called and asked Dad to help with his water pump. Dad and Mom had a shouting match about my dad's being at everyone's beck and call. I was surprised to hear her say, "Raphael, you always leave whatever you are doing to help them. Where were they when you needed help picking corn last fall?" I would leave the house when they argued. Although I agreed with Mom most of the time, I didn't want to miss the chance to go with Dad to help the neighbors.

My parents constantly struggled about his willingness to stop everything and assist others. She was a stiletto in going to the quick about what he should do. His role was to mollify her stabs and mediate. The neighbors saw him as the good guy and my mother as an obstructionist.

Once two neighborhood brothers stopped at our farm to buy eggs. Commenting on my mother, one said to the other, "Raphael is a nice guy, but Gerene is a b----." He deliberately spoke loudly enough so Mom would hear it. If I had been older, I would have given him a piece of my mind and shown him my fist. My mother seldom showed her feelings. Once she stated her opinion, it was hard for her to change her mind or apologize. Some people disliked her because of this trait. When she heard that neighbor's nasty comment, she bit her lip and never sold him another egg.

Mom came to my rescue when I disagreed with Dad. She saved me from getting a bottom warming once when I forgot to herd the cows. She told Dad she had asked me to work in the garden. She found a way to help me more than once. I always felt Mom came to my rescue when I got in trouble. But she always respected Dad.

My mother used her own past as a model to guide me. I always liked listening to her talk about her nursing career. Describing how she worked with the doctors intrigued me. She reminded me to create a future, as she had when she was my age. Caught in the confines of her own life, she set goals for us children. She controlled the checkbook and sacrificed modernizing the kitchen to ensure there was money for school.

The farm finances created a tug of war between my parents. Dad got his machinery; we got school essentials. While constantly bickering about when she would get her new stove, she waited patiently for other kitchen improvements. These feisty disputes between them benefited me. She always found money for me for books and school needs. My mother's determination for her children's education opened a whole new vista for me. When referring to her challenges when she went to school, she would say, "If I did it in my time, you can do better."

Children my age in Asbury focused on farm planting and growing methods. Only two families emphasized educational growth: the Houstons and us. The Houston's oldest son, Martin, later observed to me, "It was our mothers who set higher goals. Although both of our fathers were good, honest men, they seemed confined by their visions. Our mothers emphasized the importance of education." Mom, along with Mrs. Houston, changed the course of our futures.

Mom lived to age 94. She dedicated her life to the farm and her children.

The Garden Ritual.... Mom's Legacy

Mom waking Dad from his noontime snooze was a daily routine in my parents' relationship. Most of the time, she lobbied him into consciousness because she wanted something done in the house or outside like preparing her garden. Every Spring Mom planned and planted her garden, an area about twice the size of the lawn surrounding the house. Drawing on her background organizing the surgery room for doctors, she stamped her ownership on every square foot of cabbage and strawberries.

Her ritual began when Dad spread fertilizer over the growing area, then plowed the rich, fallow earth for a new growing season. After Dad and I used a hoe and garden rake to break up the larger clumps of earth, she carefully prepared the ground for seeds and sprouts. Dad used to grumble to me, "Your mother always makes this garden too big!" Mom carefully sectioned off the garden for various growing plants and reserved the right corner for cucumbers, squash, and watermelon. Because these vegetables developed long, creeping vines, they needed a lot of space. Later, one of my tasks was cutting and removing weeds growing among the vines.

Mom showed me how to use the hoe's edge to create planting rows. We planted a long row of carrot seeds in the middle area of the garden. Here, in the soft, less compacted earth the carrot could push its way down. In addition to carrots, we planted beets, scallions, string beans and cabbage in nicely sculptured rows. We did an early planting of sweet corn in rows side by side so the corn could pollinate and produce ears by the fourth of July. We planted tomatoes, lettuce and spinach in the front part of the garden near the house so they could be gathered easily for every meal .

I always liked garden work. While hoeing the soil, I imagined the taste of a freshly pulled carrot. I tolerated other farm work. I knew those crops were necessary for the animals, but I preferred working for my own fresh plate of lettuce, potatoes and beans.

A maze of dill, grapes and strawberries spread across the left side of the garden up to the fence. The fence prevented the chickens from sticking their beaks through the wire holes and sampling the garden delicacies. When the grapes ripened, I would snatch a bunch. Mom noticed the missing grapes, but she never caught me and must have concluded some animal had eaten them. The garden was the horticultural plot of land that my mother claimed and tended. Each day walking among the plentiful, lush plants, she would stop, pull a few weeds and announce, "The lettuce is ready; the spinach needs more time."

I believe half the town of Asbury benefited from my mother's plentiful garden. As visitors came to buy their eggs, they somehow also left with a bag full of tomatoes, cucumbers, beans, or whatever the "giving garden" had produced. She would choose a new variety of vegetable as her favorite food each summer, often "canning" it into countless jars for winter consumption. One summer, eggplants caught her fancy. We had fried eggplant for breakfast, eggplant sandwiches for lunch, and baked parmesan for dinner. I ate too much eggplant that summer. I looked in the mirror one night and through the blurred lighting, it appeared my face was the deep purple shade of an eggplant. To this day I cannot eat eggplant, disguised, seasoned, parmesan or whatever.

Two great inventions for my mother included the pressure cooker and ball jars with lids that sealed. The pressure cooker, a canning devotee's dream, lived up to its name, transforming turgid, rigid vegetables into softer, edible entities. Tomatoes, beets, or other foods became "soup-like," easily packed into the ball jars. The heat from the steam pressure created a vacuum in the jars, locking in the freshness for many months. These tightly sealed jars prevented decay during storage. I can still see my mother standing in the kitchen, hesitantly reaching, unlatching and lifting the pressure cooker lid as a cascade of steam engulfed her. She used forceps to slowly lift each jar from the cooker, then carefully placed the caps on the jars to seal them before they cooled. Finally, she'd wind on a ringed cap to keep the sealed cover in place.

She performed this ritual throughout the summer as various vegetables ripened. Michigan grown peaches were her favorite for canning fruit. No matter the temperature, when the plants ripened, she canned. Believe me, on some summer days, the temperature was so hot, she probably didn't need the pressure cooker. We stored all the canned goods in the cellar on shelves along the basement walls. Although I don't recall the number of shelves or quart jars, all of us enjoyed "garden food" for the fall, winter and spring days. As if by magic, the jars were always emptied and readied for the next summer's canning process.

My love for vegetables stems from years of fresh farm produce and succulent jars of canned vegetables. My mother tilled the soil and supplied Asbury with fresh vegetables from our garden of Eden. Most of all, she provided sustenance for seven growing children.

CHAPTER 14

My Father's Parents Help Populate Northeast Iowa

My paternal grandparents, Nick and Anna Freiburger, were in a biblical sense, the start of a genealogical kingdom. They had 14 children, who married and created a generational population explosion. By 2015, I was one of 300 relations at a family reunion of Nick and Anna's descendants. They lived in a small town called Sageville, Iowa, just outside Dubuque. It was a short ride from my home in Asbury.

Nick and Anna Freiburger
November 13, 1906 – Holy Cross, Iowa

Asbury to Sageville Map

I did not know my grandmother very well. I remember her as a tall woman with a prominent goiter caused by a dysfunctional thyroid. She was diabetic and suffered from a heart condition. I usually spent time with my grandfather when I wasn't playing with cousins during our visits. Whenever I visited their house on Sundays, it was swarming with my father's siblings, spouses, and offspring. These visits were filled with stories, singing and a lot of teasing.

Being one of the oldest of the grandchildren, I was privileged to hear Grampa tell stories. He spun many a yarn about the good old days. He had a different perspective of the world than most, and he refused to change it. Until his death, he believed the earth was flat and despite watching it on TV, maintained that the moon landing was a hoax.

My grandfather served in many roles. He was a barber when he married Ann. As the children were born, he took on the roles of a farmer of 347 acres, a sawmill operator, and a blacksmith. In his leisure time he was the mayor of the town of Sageville and played the fiddle at town dances and gatherings.

During his prodigious progenitor role, Grampa Nick and my dad carved out a close relationship. They retained this strong relationship even in Grampa's older years. He wanted my father at his side during every important crisis of health. When he sold the farm in his mid-60s and bought a house in Dubuque, my father was the one who helped him make the decision. He singled out Dad from among his children to "take care of his money when he died."

Dad clearly inherited his storytelling skills from his father, and as a boy, I often would sit for hours listening to them spin their tales. When sharpening a saw, Dad would stop and tell me he was using the file exactly as his father had taught him. As a young boy, I tried to follow my father's example and do things just as Dad did. They were my childhood heroes. One day when Dad showed me how to put hinges on a door, I pictured my father in the same role that Grampa Nick played for him.

My grandmother died of a heart attack on February 6, 1951, when I was 13 years old. My mother, in her role as a nurse, tended to her in her final illness. Although we had a neighbor girl come and cook, I remember praying that Gramma would die so Mom could return home to us kids. The neighbor girl Dad hired to cook and keep house was nice, but I really missed Mom's food and attention. I felt bad for her; I think she knew what I was thinking.

My grandfather married Loretta Crimmins in the 1980s and became the stepfather of seven more kids. In the 1990s when the City of Dubuque conducted a contest to find the grandfather who had the most grandchildren, Grampa Nick won by a margin of 20, with his and Loretta's grandchildren.

After I moved away, I always tried to stop by to visit Grampa Nick. On one visit I found my 90-year-old grandfather out in the garage wearing his carpenter apron, the ever-present bow tie, garters on his forearm shirt sleeves, and his favorite hat. He stopped his work and came over to show off his latest creation, a doghouse.

This doghouse was a pet designer's dream. It had the traditional entry opening on one end. On the back side were sliding doors, opening to a carpeted interior. The roof was meticulously shingled, and there was an attic window in the end opposite the dog entry opening. The exterior was neatly sided and painted. This work of art was the second ordered by a Chicago customer.

Grampa had put up a sign on the street in front of the house. I surmised the lady from Chicago had seen the sign while driving by on a visit to Dubuque and bought her first doghouse. I also believe it was that sign that developed a word of mouth marketing approach, leading to an increase in buyers. He laughed as he told me that twice a week, he went to the city dump and gathered the boards he needed to build the houses. He would then pick up the hammer, a small finishing hammer with claws, and talk about its history. He pointed to a spot on the slender handle where he had placed a nail to hold the split in the handle together.

"I put in that nail 50 years ago and it is still holding," and with a sly smile, he continued, "This hammer is 75 years old, and it isn't even rusty." As he continued his story, he drifted into describing the lady who was coming to pick up the doghouse over the weekend. He said she had bought one earlier and had come to pick it up in her car. He laughed heartily when he began talking about loading the doghouse into the trunk of her car. "First, we had to measure and make sure it would fit. Then we had the problem of lifting it up and into the trunk."

He gave a detailed rendition: "I told her we would each have to lift one end when we put the doghouse in the car trunk. Then we slid it over to the car. I explained that she would have to get her hands under the bottom edge. It was too heavy for her to lift and put her hands underneath at the same time, so I went to her end, helping her lift it high enough to get her hands underneath. Then I shifted to the other end and lifted my end. As we began to move toward the car trunk, she made a whopping, big fart. We both got to laughing so much, we had to put the doghouse down and start over. Eventually, we managed to hold the laughter (and the gas) and lift the doghouse into the trunk."

Grampa's stories delighted me, and I had so many more questions, but at some point, he would tell me, "I have to go back to work."

One day, however, Grampa had to answer unexpected questions. Unannounced, the building inspector arrived and began asking questions. It seems that a neighbor complained to the city that Nick Freiburger was building without a permit. My grandfather was up to the challenge. He explained how he gathered the materials, showed a sample doghouse he had constructed, and asked a question of his own: "Why would anyone be upset about me creating such fashionable homes for dogs?" The inspector heartily agreed and said he had no problem with Nick's future construction of dog houses. Grampa did just that, continuing until he was 96 and had built 100 of them. He only stopped because he couldn't drive, and no one had time to take him to the dump to collect materials. He teasingly said the income from his works of art was "beer money" for Loretta, his wife.

Grampa Nick was a legendary guest at his 100th birthday party when my father and several of his siblings gathered at the assisted living residence. Grampa joined them all in singing "Happy Birthday" and helped blow out the candles on the cake. As they were leaving, my father overheard him ask the attendant nurse, "Who were those people? They seemed to be having a good time." Grampa Nick died June 20,1989, at the age of 104. I will always remember him as the 96-year-old storyteller and the builder of "fashionable" dog houses. In his will he remembered me and each of his grandchildren. I received a check in the amount of $14.75. I can see him raising his gartered arm and pointing at me and saying, "Use the money to buy a bologna sandwich and come join me for lunch."

CHAPTER 15

My Mother's Panther Creek Roots

"There's a long, long trail a winding to the land of my... grandparents." For me, the drive from our home in Asbury, to Panther Creek in North Buena Vista. Iowa, was that long, long trail.

Asbury to Buena Vista map

North Buena Vista was nestled in a valley under a prominent bluff overlooking the Mississippi river, hence its name "beautiful view." When my grandparents were alive two taverns, a Catholic Church, and a few houses comprised the town. My uncle Joe's home housed the post office.

We drove the road which snaked about two miles along Panther Creek back into a hidden valley. In the springtime it was a sparsely traveled muddy road. I remember passing the homes of the Bakulas and the Rinikers and then after what appeared to be an eternity. Finally arriving proved to be an adventure. We had to ford Panther Creek to cross over to their home. In the spring when the snow thawed, the water was often deep. Fortunately, our Model A Ford had a high clearance, and we could drive it through up to a foot and a half of flowing water.

On drier land we were greeted by wooden ducks with swiveling wings flying on the garden fence posts. Both of my grandfathers were builders, but Grandfather Charlie lived in an area known for barn building. At least half of the barns in a 50-mile radius had his name on the corner timber. His carpentry also included building many homes on the local farms.

In 1934, Nick and Anna Freiburger hired Charlie Bauer to build a new house on their farm. This was an early connection between the Bauers and Freiburgers, both of whom would eventually become my grandparents.

While Charlie Bauer was building their house, Anna Freiburger, who had diabetes and a heart condition, became ill. Nick told Charlie they were looking for a nurse to sit with his ill wife. Charlie informed Nick he had a daughter who was a nurse and might be available. They hired that nurse who became my mother, Gerene Bauer, to care for Anna.

During Gerene's stay as Anna's nurse, one of Nick's sons, my father, Raphael, had an eye for her. Feeling she was special, he decided to ask her for a date. He arrived one evening with a bouquet of wildflowers at the home where Gerene was staying. He knocked at the door, and when the owner, Rose Ahrendt, answered, he stood hat in hand with the flower bouquet, and asked to see Miss Bauer.

It was my father and mother's first date. After a year of courting, they married in January, 1936. A year later I was born. The elder Freiburgers and Bauers became my grandparents.

As an artisan woodworker, Grampa Bauer taught woodworking in the Dubuque schools. In his barn workshop. He carved and completed a whole host of decorative wood items, he always sent wooden trinkets and toys home when we visited. I enjoyed many a run in the snow on a wooden sled he made. My brother Mike's grandchildren still play with the small hip-roofed barn Grampa made.

Grampa Bauer handcrafted a cedar chest for my mother. Beautifully finished, the exterior surface accentuates the lines in the cedar wood. My daughter Maria now treasures it as an antique.

I also remember when we arrived at their house, Grampa would come out in his striped overalls, shuffle over to the car, and welcome us. He called my mother "G'ne" and always gave her a hug. My grandmother, dressed in her long skirt, shawl and long brown stockings, would eventually emerge to greet us.

Once we settled in the house, we also settled into its ritual. Gramma gave a quick catch-up on the news of everyone in the family and their neighbors in the valley. Then Grampa would parade his toys and gimmicks. He had a "Charlie Weaver" animated drinking toy, which shook a mixing cup for drinks and shot out a Fourth of July display of sparkling lights. His, also my, favorite mischief was a statuette of a boy walking a dog by a lamppost. Attached was a rubber squeeze bulb filled with water. He would hold the statuette with the dog in front of me and squeeze the bulb; the dog would lift its leg and a stream of water would squirt out. On every visit, the dog relieved himself on every one of us.

Another ever-present toy was a bird that would keep bobbing its head in a glass of water. Eventually during our visit, Grampa would come over to me, give me a big smile, and reach out to shake hands. Slyly he would slip a clump of realistic Plaster of Paris dog poop in my hand. Even though I knew it wasn't real, I'd put it down and wipe my hands. This parade of his gadgets continued during each visit.

On our Christmas visits, Grampa served Tom and Jerrys, his specialty. The drink is a mix of rum, egg nog, sugar, and vanilla. I can still see him putting a couple of spoonsful of the mixture in a mug, adding rum, pouring in hot water from the teakettle into the mug, swishing it with a spoon and adding a shake of cinnamon on top. His elderly callused hands would shake as he served each adult the drink.

I was always fascinated when their phone rang. The telephone was a wooden box mounted on the kitchen wall. It had a projecting black nozzle into which you could speak, and an earpiece shaped like a butternut squash with a long cord hanging on the side of the box. To answer or calling you lifted the earpiece from the holder. The phone was a party line. Each customer had a code of rings. The number of rings revealed who was on the phone

There was a crank on the box used to do the ringing. My grandparents' number was four long rings, and two shorts. While we were visiting, I would sit near the phone, hoping it might ring.

The whole valley and town were connected to the telephone line strung on poles along the road. If my grandparents wanted to call us, they would ring the town operator, one crank, and she would use her switchboard to place the call through to us. The party line served as a newspaper for all the neighbors. This is how everyone in the neighboring area kept up to date on births, deaths and, of course, gossip.

My grandparents' house had a porch entry in front, and I remember a distinct smell, kind of a musty, vinegary odor when entering. I never could determine its source. We spent most of our time in the kitchen, also serving as a dining room, and the cooking aroma displaced the entry way odor.

My Bauer grandparents lived in Dubuque for many years and Grampa's sister, Irma, had also lived in Dubuque for many years. Legend has it that Grampa Charlie and Irma's husband, Art, had a spat, prompting my grandparents' move to Buena Vista. All their other relatives were located around the original birthplaces on the Turkey River in northeast Iowa or Prairie du Chien, Wisconsin. I could never understand why they moved from the city to such an isolated place. When I would ask my mother about the move, she would give me a silent glare.

My Grampa Charlie was very jovial, sociable. He had spent time as a logger in the Northwest rainforests before marriage and traveled in the Northeastern states. Mom had some of his spirit of adventure when she left home at 12 to live with her grandparents in Monona, Iowa.

Working alone away from home was a continuing pattern in my Grandfather's life. He stayed with the families for whom he did carpentry and was away from home a lot, a reality putting the parenting burden on my grandmother. She became a strong matriarch, held the family reins, and raised my mother and her siblings.

Years later when we visited, or were with my grandparents, she was the audience for Grampa's stories. She would sit in her rocking chair, chuckle and shake her head from side to side as he humorously rattled on.

All three daughters held their wedding receptions at the Bauer house on Panther Creek. My parents' wedding album features a picture of them standing on a clothesline platform by the Panther

Creek house at their reception. The platform was built by Grampa Charlie and served the role of photography studio on this January day when the ground was snow covered.

My Parents Wedding Day
Left to right: Dad, Mom, Father Schmitt, Anastasia (Dad's sister and bridesmaid), and Charlie Bauer Jr. (Mom's brother and best man)
January 14, 1936

When Mom's youngest sister, Irma, got married, Marvin Petsche, as groom, was responsible for alcoholic drinks at the wedding reception. Beer by the case was very scarce. I was excited to accompany him and Dad, as we had to go to four different taverns to get enough cases of beer. I attended the wedding reception held under the spreading willow tree in their back yard along Panther Creek.

When Grampa and Grandma Bauer had health issues in their later years, they came and stayed at our home in Asbury. My mother was obsessed with the fact that Grampa had not attended church for many years. She asked our local pastor to reconvert him. Grampa went to confession and communion and was a church goer in his remaining days. It was a great relief to Mom, who had said many a prayer that he would return to church and have a Christian burial.

Margaret and Charlie Bauer, my maternal grandparents
celebrating their 50th anniversary
1960

I always remember my maternal grandparents and their Panther Creek home. Our visits were mostly on holidays and were always heartwarming to me. They are both resting in peace in a cemetery overlooking the Mississippi River. There they will eternally enjoy a "Buena Vista."

CHAPTER 16

My Adopted Grandparents

"Call it a clan, call it a network, call it a tribe, or call it a family. Whatever you call it, whoever you are, you need one."

~ Jane Howard

We are all born into families with generations of relations. But special people can often become what I call "real relations" although not blood relatives. When I think of Rose and Bill Ahrendt, I am talking about "real relations."

Rose and Bill Ahrendt; Tom and me Circa 1940

Bill and Rose became fixtures in my life by the time I was two years old. Somewhere in a Dubuque neighborhood, Bill and Rose met up with my grandparents, Charles and Margaret Bauer. The friendship continued to grow through geographical moves and decades.

That friendship led my mother daughter of the Bauers, to re-connect with the Ahrendts. While pursuing her nursing degree at Mercy Hospital, and she moved in with them. My father's knock at their door led to the courtship and marriage of my parents. The friendship was now linked to another generation of Freiburgers.

As a very little guy, I remember Bill and Rose coming to visit the farm to buy eggs and visit my parents. I always liked Bill. He told me stories and showed me how all the instruments on his new Plymouth car worked. On one occasion when Dad threatened to spank me for not closing the hen house door and letting the chickens out, Bill said, "Raphael, it wasn't that bad. Be easy on him."

When Bill visited, he made me feel special because he always brought something for me. Rose would later pick up in the same ritual with my sister, Margaret. My two brothers Don and Tom were also close to Bill, but not as close as I was.

From early on I created some drama and excitement when Bill and Rose visited. One drama entailed a search. At four-years old, I had decided to strike out with my younger brother Tom to float sticks in the meandering creek through the cow pasture on our farm. It turned out our adventure followed the creek for quite a distance. It took my Dad, Mom, Bill and Rose almost an hour to find us.

When they arrived, Dad helped Tom, his clothes totally soaked, out of the creek. As his bossy older brother, I had made him walk in the creek to float the sticks.

I will never forget Mom looking ahead where the creek became a deep pool, and turning to Bill and Rose said, "Oh my God, I am so glad we found these two before they got to that pool."

Other exploits were more mundane. We had an engine, one cylinder, to pump the water from the well. A belt ran from the engine to the pump, and when the holding tank was low, my father would start the engine and pump water until the tank was filled. Because the water was often pumped sometimes a couple of times a day, the belt became shiny and started slipping. To make the belt stick to the pulleys, Dad applied tar to the belt with a stick. He put the stick in the can of tar and while the belt was running, dropped tar from the stick on the inner surface of the belt.

Being a keen four-year-old observer of this whole procedure, I took my brother Tom out to pump water. I figured out how to crank and start the engine. I succeeded in tarring not only the belt but also the two of us. Just as I had tarred up the belt, Bill and Rose arrived. I still remember Bill laughing as he was rubbing the cloth covered with distillate, the fuel for the tractor, and cleaning the tar from my arms and face. My mother was so angry, she wouldn't talk to me. She focused mightily on cleaning up Tom. Unfortunately, we either did not have cameras, or my mother didn't want to use one. My memory is the only picture I have of that caper.

When we moved from the Craig farm to the Wernimont farm, I had another episode of mischievousness. I was now five years old and enrolled in kindergarten at the Julien School. My best friend was a girl my age, Shirley Waters.

The school had a small enrollment, maybe ten. Other than Shirley, the only people I remember were two older girls who used to play with me at recess. I was fascinated by a pair of eighth grade fraternal twins who smoked corncob pipes at recess. Because they were older, the teacher did not interfere with their smoking habits.

After school one day, Shirley told me that her neighbors had a new baby. We went over to the house and asked if we could see him. Well, Mrs. Cain welcomed us and got out some milk and cookies. We had the greatest visit for at least an hour and a half.

Again, Bill and Rose had stopped at our farm to buy some eggs. I usually walked the mile and a half home after school along a state highway but this day, my parents didn't know about my baby visiting.

When I didn't arrive after an hour, my tardiness conjured up some frightful visions. Mom and the Ahrendts became concerned and set out to find me. As I came out of the Cain house, the aroma of homemade cookies on my clothes, I was surprised to see Bill driving the car slowly along the road. Mom and Rose were walking and checking both sides of the road. The first ten seconds were filled with elation when they saw me walk out of the Cain house. Then Mom shoved me into the car, and I didn't have a very happy evening after Bill and Rose left. I never heard anything about Shirley's late arrival home. I was happy, though, that Bill and Rose had spared me from getting my bottom warmed. They always seemed to "save" me, so that was yet another reason I was always happy to see them driving down our lane after Bill's long workday delivering mail.

A woman named Gertie lived in one of the homes on his mail delivery route and gave Bill a cat. Bill brought her to our farm, and we named her Gertie. She became my favorite pet.

Bill also loved dogs. On one occasion he brought a black Labrador retriever out to the farm for us to temporarily house him. We put him in the barn and tied him to a bale of hay. He was an extremely people-oriented dog. One day after tying the dog to the bale, I went out the barn door, stopped and looked behind to see him running and dragging the bale toward me.

As I grew older, Bill took me under his wing. He taught me how to hunt, mostly rabbits and pheasants. On my tenth birthday he gave me a pocketknife—a real super-duper model with a can opener and carving blade, a prototype of the Swiss Army knife. Now I felt grown up like Dad. I had my own knife when fixing things on the farm.

My overalls, worn from long term use, had a hole in the pocket. One day the pocketknife fell through the hole. I mourned the loss by imagining that I had planted it, and I would find a "pocketknife tree" the next spring. After a year or so when Bill asked about the knife, I would tell him I kept it by my bed for fear of losing it, too embarrassed to tell him I had lost it. Mom told me never to tell him; she thought he would feel he had to buy me another knife.

When I was twelve, Bill and Rose cheered me on when I had to take the eighth-grade tests to enter high school. At report card time my parents would share my grades with Bill and Rose and point out my deportment grade, my worst score. The Ahrendts always reminded them, "Look at the good grades in the other subjects. Don't just focus on deportment." Saved by the Ahrendts once again!

I have happy memories of Bill and Rose. If as the saying goes, nobody can do for little children what grandparents do, Rose and Bill were, indeed, my adopted grandparents. While they were not related to our family by birth, Bill and Rose became "real relations."

CHAPTER 17

The Neighbors

The Batton families were prominent because they owned six farms in the community. Three of their farms formed boundaries around our 160 acres of land. Known by all as "Uncle" Jacob, he was considered the patriarch of the families and owned one of the bordering farms. The other bordering fence lines belonged to his nephews, Denis and Clarence.

The Battons had Westphalian roots. Active Democrats, Denis and Mike were elected to the Board of Supervisors for Dubuque County. Considered important members of the Asbury community, the Battons claimed their family had founded and built St. Philomena's church.

The Bishop assigned Father John Neuman as pastor of St. Philomena's in the late 50s to build a Catholic elementary school. After failed attempts to purchase land on a farm adjoining the church property, he found a new site about a mile down the road on the Welter farm. This decision meant the church would have to move to the new site.

The Battons objected, protesting loudly that they had not been consulted about the move. Father Neuman told them, "I am in charge and I will do what the Bishop tells me, whether you agree or not." Resisting him and the change of site, the Battons convened a meeting at the fire station to organize those opposed to the move. Demonstrating their defiance, they stopped attending St Philomena's and drove past the church on Sundays to attend Mass elsewhere.

Asbury's firehouse, next to Horton's Store, became a regular meeting place for the dissenters. They invited my parents to their meetings. Dad and Mom insisted that the need for a school was the important issue and refused to join their meetings, and they remained loyal to Father Neuman.

Denis Batton, one of the more vocal dissenters, demonstrated his resentment towards my parents on more than one occasion. Several times visitors to our farm told my parents he despised them for supporting Father Neuman in tearing down his church. The fence between our two farms served both as a physical boundary and a line of demarcation between the opposing views. On one occasion Denis called my father out for supporting the new church. He refused to speak to my father until years after the new school and church, Church of the Resurrection, were built and a new pastor assigned. Denis apologized to my parents for his behavior. He accepted and attended the new parish.

Unfortunately, rural community feuds of this nature occurred often. Owning a farm sparks a special kind of proprietorship. As a youngster I was fascinated by the different brands of farm machinery used on neighboring farms. Often in conversations between my Dad and other owners, I heard claims that Farmall tractors were better than my father's John Deere. Like my father, my favorite was John Deere. Such things as breeds of cows or machinery provoked discussion, sometimes arguments, but, despite the minor jealousies and disagreements, friendships, for the most part, trumped cows and tractors.

My parents never got caught up in these personalized disputes. As I recall, my brothers and sisters and I never were caught up in community quarrels either. Even if I was a John Deere fan, when arguing with one of the neighbor kids, I acknowledged Farmalls as my second choice. Like our parents, my siblings and I tried to stay friends with everyone in school.

People who visited our farm left on friendly terms. More frequently they also left with vegetables, eggs or homemade bread from my mother. My father also was one of the first on the scene when someone in the community needed help. Our farm displayed proprietorship, but our fences were built to keep out stray animals, not erected to serve as a line of demarcation for "a personal grudge" against others.

4-H Club

When I was twelve years old, the neighborhood parents met in our home to form a 4-H club. They selected my father as the adult club leader. The club met monthly in the homes of the members. After the meetings, the host family provided a lunch or snack. The Gladwin's home was a curiosity. They spoke German in their house. I remember in the middle of a 4-H meeting in their home hearing Mr. Gladwin say "Aus mit der Kat," a German expression for take the cat out of the house. The meeting came to an abrupt stop and there was a period of silent wonderment. Everyone was stunned by the German expression. None of us had ever heard a language other than English in Asbury. Their son, whom we called Junior, was a member of the 4-H club. For some unknown reason, I don't think anyone ever talked to him about his parents and their language. I, and all the club members felt he was embarrassed because they spoke German.

The 4-H symbol stands for head, heart, hands and health. The 4-H motto was "to make the best better." I had a running debate with one of the club members about the motto. He argued it should read "to make the better best." I won when the official t-shirts arrived with my preference, "to make the best better." Dad told me later he agreed with me.

The monthly meetings involved activity reports and discussions focused on the motto and the 4-H symbol. Members would report on the progress of their projects, most of which were preparing animals for the annual fair. In the second year of my 4-H club membership, the Purina feed representative, Leonard Wolfe, gave me a female pig for my project. The program was called "Mike and Ike." I was excited but realized I had to learn record keeping and write a final report. I asked Mom to help me organize the record pages.

I kept daily records of the amount of the feed, the gain in weight, and the care I gave the pig in preparation for the county fair. At the fair, I displayed the records, so that the judge could review them. The judge closely examined the pig's head, ears and rib area and checked the weight chart in my records. I was totally amazed when he called me forward and handed me both a blue and grand champion ribbon.

Tom, David Batton, and me admiring my 4-H pig - 1948

After the fair, my pig was bred and delivered a litter of six piglets. I returned one of the them to the Purina rep the next year and sold the remaining five for my personal profit. The earnings from the sale paid the tuition for my freshman year in high school. I learned record keeping; developed the responsibility of caring for an animal; and acquired the ability to calculate costs, sales, and profits. After the fair I sat one evening and reviewed my record keeping. I really had learned a lot. It was fun being a pig owner. In quiet times I would dream about owning my own farm and raising pigs.

Willem's School Project

I told many stories about the farm to my grandsons. Having heard the stories, Willem, chose the State of Iowa for a class project in school. Fortunately, I had saved the records of my pig project. When people came to his project, he told them the story of my pig and showed them my records displayed at his exhibit.

Willem, my grandson, presenting his fourth grade geography project on the State of Iowa, 2015.

CHAPTER 18

Pranksters in the Neighborhood

Throughout the Asbury Community we did have a good mix of eccentric characters. The Knutson family qualified for the most unconventional behavior. They were a large family, with sons totally unsupervised by the parents. The eldest son was arrested for stealing a car and crashing it. He ended up in Anamosa State Prison, creating a delinquency pattern for his four younger brothers. My parents made every effort to keep us separated from the Knutson kids. Although the two oldest boys, three to five years older than me, didn't pay me much attention, I had to resort to fisticuffs to gain the respect of Ronnie and Willie, who were my age.

The Knutsons caught the attention of the school nurse when they introduced impetigo, red sores on the face and mouth, to the all at school. I looked around one day and saw the telltale gentian violet smears used to cure the disease, on almost everyone.

Four of the younger brothers wandered shoeless around the neighborhood, doing their Huck Finn kind of mischief. Unstocked cupboards in their own house motivated them to pillage every apple orchard, fruit tree, and garden in a three-mile radius. They did odd jobs in the neighborhood for food. Dad had them cut thistles and paid them with a dinner cooked by Mom.

My favorite Knutson antic was their taming of Clarence Batton's bull. When we were driving home one day, we saw one of them riding the bull, another leading the bull by the ring in his nose, and a third walking behind, prodding the animal with a large stick. Later they told me, "We tamed the bull. When we finished, he was tired and laid down to rest. We left him puffing in the pasture."

The Battons, Knutsons, my siblings and I formed a motley pack walking home after school. As a distraction from the boring walk, we tried to come up with something exciting to do during the two-mile trek. Some of those "distractions" involved annoying neighbors along the way.

Orville Peacock was a victim of one of those pranks. As we walked by his house we would try to torment him. His house was a saltbox with a long, slanting roof facing toward the road. If we did not see him, we would throw rocks up on the roof. Orville inevitably came out of a nearby shed or barn with a pitchfork pointed at us, shouting, "If I ever catch who is throwing those rocks, I will use this pitchfork on him." We'd race away to avoid his wrath. He knew us, but he never told any of our parents.

Another neighbor on our path, Mrs. Arnsdorf, had a well-kept orchard. Two of the trees stood right along the road without a fence as a barrier. We eagerly watched the apples turn to an enticing red, and then made our move. After one successful raid, she met us on our second attempt with a vicious-looking dog who charged and barked threateningly at us. The remainder of the fall we would salivate, looking from a distance at the apples, but we stayed out of the tree, fearful of that dog.

Apples were not our only targets; we also found cookies. Jim Hilliard was the janitor at our church. He, and his wife, and their parrot lived in a large gray shingled house right on the edge of the road where we walked. His wife would sit in the window facing the street, wave at us, and hold up a cookie. When we saw it, we would go over, pretending to visit the parrot. The cookies were worth the visit; her cookies were more of an attraction than a conversation with the parrot. My parents were not aware of those and many other acts of mischief. But one merited their and my pastor's attention.

Poles with large insulators holding the telephone and electric wires lined the road where we walked. My siblings, the Knutsons, and the Battons created a contest to see who could hit the most insulators with stones. I won many of those contests, repeatedly hitting the most insulators. I was proud of my throwing arm. Often, I would wander off alone throwing rocks from our lane at the fence posts and pretend I was a baseball pitcher like Bob Feller.

When the broken insulators were reported, the electric company started weekly inspections of the lines. The linemen making the repairs concluded someone was throwing rocks at the insulators. When doing some electric work at the Church, they asked Father Long if he had any idea who might be throwing the rocks.

Shortly after, the pastor when meeting with a group of us stated, "Someone is throwing rocks at the electric insulators, and the Knutsons aren't the only ones who walk home from school on that road." No one confessed. My sense of remorse was not strong enough to confess that I'd broken some of the insulators. Also, I didn't want my parents to have to pay for them. He knew some of us were throwing the rocks but did not tell the electric company.

Local Legends

When I was not rock throwing or busy with other pranks, two fellas piqued my curiosity: Mike Herndon and Marty Berens. Mike was a seasoned tobacco chewer and had the most elastic jaws I have ever seen. I used every possible ploy to engage him in storytelling. He chewed with such a vengeance that he did not have to spit. The tobacco "juice" went down the sides of his mouth onto his shirt, all the way down creating brown avenues on his overalls. I nicknamed him "juicy jaws!" I marveled that he could keep his jaws in motion chewing and talking at the same time. Marty Berens's little farmhouse stood right across the fence from the boy's outdoor toilet at the school. When I went to the bathroom, I would sneak a look over the fence to see what Marty was doing that day. Often, he was sitting, talking to himself while holding a bottle of beer. Marty seemed to be a 24/7 consumer of beer, always from the same Dubuque Star beer case.

This was the real Asbury where I grew up. While it was no Brigadoon when I lived there, little of what I have described remains. The farm where I was raised is now a suburb of 200 houses. The school is an ice cream parlor. The gravel road on which I walked to school is blacktopped.

Returning after more than 60 years, I found nothing familiar. I paused and summoned up a scene from the past. I stopped on the road near the Protestant cemetery where in days gone by I used to see in the distance the towering pine trees surrounding the farm where I lived. Now in front of me is a ranch house blocking my view. Not only have I aged, but both my hometown and I have gone through many different stages. It might not have been an exciting place, but I did know that I loved Asbury.

CHAPTER 19

Lightning Strikes Twice

Most Iowa summer days were hot and muggy. On any day, the sky darkened, and within a few minutes a raging thunderstorm would fill the sky with lightning and thunder. Rods were placed on the roofs of buildings to capture the bolts of lightning. Frequently, the lightning struck one of the tall pines forming a grove around the farm buildings. A lightning bolt strike on one of those trees led to a tall tale Dad loved to tell about good friends, Andy and Marie Steffes.

They were well intentioned people and made frequent visits to the farm. On one of those visits, Dad hooked up the horses under a tall pine as Andy arrived. Andy called Dad's attention to a missing strip of bark removed all the way up the pine's trunk by a lightning strike. "Raphael, what happened to that tree? Look at the bark."

Without hesitation, Dad said, "Andy, I walked behind Dick, the big horse you see here. I don't know what I did, but Dick kicked me so hard I bounced against the tree. It shook so hard the bark came loose."

Andy stammered, "That must have really hurt! Were you OK?"

Of course, we laughed at the exchange and Dad had a good story to add to his repertoire.

Lightning didn't confine itself to the pine trees. It struck one day when Dad and my brothers Tom, Don, and I were working on a fence in the grove. All I remember is doing a somersault and landing on my back. I looked across the road into the pasture and tried to laugh at the pigs, struck by the same lightning, lying on their backs snorting and oinking. From the house Mom had seen the lightning bolt, the pigs jump, and me falling to the ground. She came running asking me to stand up and checking my pulse. She smiled, "Everything seems okay." I was feeling a bit woozy, but I assured her I was OK. Even our Philco radio in the kitchen was smoking, also a victim of the lightning bolt. That experience led me to be careful and seek cover when future thunderstorms occurred.

Lightning was not my only concern. I was beginning to hint I might not follow in my father's footsteps. One day when I was repairing some fencing, Dad came over to me. "You're not stretching the wire right. The way you do things, you'll never be a good farmer." I threw down the hammer.

"I don't want to be a farmer like you. All you do is make hay and build stupid fences." He told me to go home and he would fix the fence right. I went home mad as a hornet. Mom told me I needed to listen and be more respectful of Dad. Now upset with her, I went out and sat on my favorite stump in the orchard.

That summer was tense. I tried to be less of smart ass storming up another cloud. And then another kind of lightning struck. Although warned of the dangers, I always believed accidents happened to other people. It was the Battons or Hortons who lost fingers or broke legs.

Countless tools and machinery required for the plantings and harvestings on our farm had speedily turning shafts and pulleys. As a young kid, always near these potential hazards, I had to be careful to avoid injury—my mother's poultices couldn't fix everything.

Before I started a task or machine, Dad would try to show me how to use a hammer safely or how to avoid my pant leg from getting caught in a turning shaft. Fortunately, neither I, nor any of my siblings, had serious injuries. When we heard of a neighbor's accident, my mother would tell us, "Thank God none of you has ever been hurt!"

Then one day I almost had a critical accident. Dad had called on me to help hitch the wagon to the tractor. The tractor lurched back and pinched my hand between the tractor drawbar and wagon hitch. The pain of that "collision" caused me to drop the hitch on my right foot. Although I was in real agony, I didn't think my father would see my pain. I was wrong.

Dad jumped off the tractor, came over, took my hand and asked, "Where did the hitch hit you?" I was totally shocked. I expected him to shout at me to be more careful. I looked up at him with tears in my eyes and said, "I'm okay." Suddenly I was looking at the relieved expression on his face and realizing how much he really cared. I survived the wagon hitch with a few minor scratches and with a lesson learned: Dad saw me as more than that young boy standing looking up at his picture on a John Deere calendar.

On that summer evening I sat under a tall pine tree listening to the cricket's call. Lightning had struck a second time in my life.

CHAPTER 20

Harvest Time and Winter Chores

In my early years the neighbors worked as a community during harvest time. They gathered with their horses and wagons to haul the corn bundles and fill silos together. I remember riding home on the wagon pulled by Dick and King, our team of horses, after a day of hauling bundles on a neighbor's farm. Joe Jaeger decided to race with us, galloping his horses past our wagon. Dad winked at me: "Hang on."

Our horses gave a snort and before we knew it, we were whizzing by that upstart team. The look of frustration on the neighbor's face as I waved good-bye speeding past his team and wagon, was unforgettable.

One by one the neighbors began hiring contractors to fill their silos. I began to feel our community shrinking from neighbors helping one another to each farmer building his own fences. As a teenager, I missed those days when neighbors had come together at harvest time.

I picked the corn with Dad. We would walk between two rows and pull the ears of corn from the stalks. When you pulled the ear out of the husk, there were sharp strands of husk that could cut the skin between your thumb and index finger. I always dreaded these cuts as they left scars as souvenirs. I wore a pick attached to a leather pad on the "husking hand," to break or cut that strand. When we picked corn, everyone had a job. My brothers Tom or Don picked up the ears that missed the wagon in the fields, and when the corn was shoveled into the crib, one of us would have to go inside and scatter the ears.

Fall was also a time of grandeur in the wooded areas of the farm. We harvested walnuts and butternuts. I enjoyed walking through the colorful display of red sumac and brown oak leaves. The cool crisp autumn morning air when I gathered the cows woke up all my senses to the beauty of living on our farm.

The green-covered walnuts turned brown after they fell to the ground for harvest. I wore gloves to hull the coverings off the walnuts because they contained an indelible stain. Even wearing gloves, my hands had yellow stains for months. Mom used the meats of the walnuts and butternuts to add a special flavor to Christmas cookies.

When all the leaves had fallen from the trees and the corn stalks stood earless, we said goodbye to fall and reluctantly accepted the coming of winter. I hated the thought of the cold wind blowing on my face and the frosty mornings when I had to do my chores.

The snow cover and cold of winter imposed a period of dormancy in our seasonal activity. Sawing wood and shoveling the lane were added to the normal care of the animals and household chores. Sawing wood for the stove and furnace was one of the most difficult of the farm chores. We usually cut firewood after the cold weather arrived when the sap was frozen in the trees and logs. While it was easier to saw them, I remember well my frozen fingers and cold feet. I detested this job. The only motivation was anticipating myself finished and thawing out while standing on the hall register (connected to the furnace below) on the bedroom level, warmed by the burning wood we had gathered. Sawing wood was not a job for the faint hearted, but when it heated the house in the winter, the memory of that chore was softened.

Dad had a portable saw attached to the front of the tractor. The saw had a table, with a saw blade approximately four feet in diameter in the middle. We drove the tractor to the site where we cut the logs into blocks which fit into the furnace.

The sawing process involved my brother Tom and me laying one end of a log on the saw table and extending the end of the log about 12 inches past the saw blade. Then Dad would push the log towards the spinning saw blade to cut a block of wood.

The most dangerous part of this process was, of course, the area around the saw. Most of the time there was snow on the ground. The snow became icy right where we were sawing. Afraid of slipping, I asked Dad to stop so that we could scatter more saw dust on the area. The saw dust helped, but we had to stop and frequently scatter more.

We took the wagon load of wood home and threw the blocks of wood into the cellar. Dad or I later went into the cellar and neatly stacked it into piles.

One winter day, shortly after I had learned to drive the tractor, we went to cut wood. I accidentally drove into a ditch and broke the front pedestal on the tractor. I was demoted, banished to stack wood while Dad drove to Waterloo with Tom to get a new pedestal.

What a terrible day for me. I was angry at myself for breaking the pedestal. I resented having to stay home. I threw wood around the basement and yelled instead of stacking it. I made such a ruckus that Mom came down to see if I was all right. She told me breaking the pedestal was not my fault.

"Then why did Dad make me stay home?" She said, "Everything will be okay when he gets the new pedestal and puts it on the tractor."

After Dad returned with the new pedestal, he let me help install it. I felt good when he examined it and said, "It looks good as new!" What a relief to me that the tractor was fixed. I went to the basement and restacked the wood, cleaning up the mess I had made—before Dad would see it.

I stood on the radiator vent and heard my father shoving another log of wood into the furnace and knew I would never forget the memory of harvesting wood. I had added it to my mental list of becoming a mailman or anything other than a farmer cutting wood or making hay.

Winter was wearisome. Chilling winds and drifting snow created blizzard conditions and snowbanks. Venturing out into this maelstrom meant snow pelted my face, and I would be trudging through deep-drifted piles with every step. The entrance lane to our farm served as a special magnet for the blowing snow. We had to shovel those drifts because they were too deep for our car to get through. Icy cheeks, stinging fingers, gloves caked with snow and ice are my memories of those shoveling experiences

On winter mornings, snuggled under my warm blankets in a room warmed by the wood we had cut, I dreaded the sight of new snow on the window. When the accompanying wind howled, I was depressed at the thought of another day of shoveling. January, February, and March seemed to last forever.

When I heard the chilling wind and saw the deep drifts, I thought about the photos of snowy scenes of New England winters on the calendars that also featured my father's picture. I'd dream of crisp blankets of clean snow where people skied and didn't have to shovel snowdrifts on cold windy days.

As a farm kid, I had special winter chores such as harnessing the horses, feeding the pigs, and milking the cows. During the colder months, I developed a whole new relationship with the farm animals. They were housed in the barn, hog house or chicken house to stay warm.

The animals had no outhouses on the farm. As the cows stood with their heads and necks in stanchions, their bums and tails were positioned over a long trough called, for good reason, the gutter. Most of the time, the measurements for the gutter were accurate, and everything fell in place. But cows sneeze and are flatulent. I accidentally walked behind a cow during one of those flatulent explosions and had an "excremental-experience." Every day we had to clean up their leavings holding our noses.

In the horse barn the stalls were designed to meet the needs of the horses who never lie down. Yes, they sleep standing up. Every day there would be a collection of "road apples" ready for collecting. The calves slept in pens. Young and untrained, they relieved themselves wherever they wanted and wherever convenient. The clean, shiny yellow straw that we had placed as a bed for them the day before radically changed color. And the pigs were the worst. Pig pen is an accurate description. Some mornings when the whiff of them coming out hit my nose, I had a change of heart about becoming a pig farmer. I felt they would be the last animals to populate my farm.

In the winter I escaped from the cold by reading books which introduced me to a whole new world outside our farm. Some days I would look for new places where I might go when I grew up.

Chapter 21

Asbury School Now Asbury Cafe

In September we interrupted the routine of our farm life to attend school. Mom paged through the Sears and Roebuck catalog to buy me a new wardrobe—shirts, overalls, and school shoes. The first week of school my parents went to the Sunbeam day-old store and stocked up on sandwich bread. I remember snitching a taste of the peanut butter, which later found its way between two slices of the bread in my lunch. When the peanut butter took its days off, I would find a fried egg sandwich wrapped in wax paper inside the brown bag. As if I were requesting lunch the next day, I carefully folded both the paper and bag, putting them in my pocket to take home after school.

All 26 Asbury kids attended the same one-room elementary school. A couple of 16-17-year-old boys, who worked during the good weather, attended school during the winter months. If I walked fast enough, I could go outside and play ball before the teacher came outside, ringing the hand-held bell.

After the opening bell, I went to my desk and plunged into my schoolwork for the day. My desktop had an opening for storing a jar of ink in the upper right-hand corner and a narrow crease along the top for pencils. I remember Mom buying me a pen that would write forever without refills to replace the fountain pen I used in school. We used wooden pencils. I frequently went to the pencil sharpener on the window in the front of the room to check out other students' projects.

The school facilities included the main building, two outdoor privies (boys and girls), a swing set with a long slide, and woodshed. One job I liked was carrying a heavy bucket of water from Mrs. Dietz's well next door each morning for drinking in the school. We had one water dispenser with paper cups in the back of the room. In the cold weather, we gathered buckets of coal and wood from the woodshed to the pot-bellied stove for heating the school. I always hoped the teacher would arrive early on cold days to stoke the stove.

We had one teacher for all the grades. I had a succession of four teachers during my seven years. The teachers were high school graduates and certified by the county superintendent, who also hired them.

My seat faced a wall with two large blackboards and white chalk sticks on their bottom shelf. Parading across the top of the blackboards were the 26 magnified letters of the alphabet, scripted in the Palmer method. They were a constant reminder of how I should shape my Ps and Qs. The painting of George Washington, as Gilbert Stuart had portrayed him, stared at us from the front wall. The American flag was prominently displayed there also.

We began each school day by standing, young ones in front, older in back, with our right hands over our hearts reciting *The Pledge of Allegiance.*

Music was scheduled once a week. The teacher put a record on the phonograph, called a Victrola, cranked it up, and placed the needle arm on the record. All the songs she played were in a key my post puberty larynx could not reach. I always felt she was upset with my singing as she glared at me while waving her arm up and down directing. We learned old songs like *"The Old Oaken Bucket"* and *"My Grandfather's Clock"* as well at the *"The Star-Spangled Banner."*

After the pledge we all read and prepared our lessons in our desks. The lower grades had workbooks.

The Victrola That Challenged My Vocal Chords

One morning when I was in the fourth grade, after the Pledge of Allegiance, Ms. Connolly held up a jetted bag, milkweed plant, ad pointed out its pods She said this plant was very important if any of our family members were serving the Army or Navy. I raised my hand and told the class my Uncle Bill was in the army and Uncle Bob in the navy, and that my grandparents had a special banner with two blue stars hanging in their living room window as a way to remember they were serving.

Ms. Connolly pointed to me and said, "Jim, you can do something special for your uncles and the other soldiers. If you find this plant on your farm, collect the pods in this special bag and bring it back to school. These pods contain a special sticky, fluffy feather-like floss used to fill life jackets. They will help soldiers like your uncles when they have to swim in the ocean." Immediately I became a milkweed pods collector to help my uncles and others.

Milkweed plants required up to three years to grow for commercial crops. The government made an unusual call for the collection of milkweed pods where t grew wild. Schoolchildren spent untold hours walking fencerows, roadsides and railroad right of ways looking for milkweeds.

I was given a netted onion sack to collect pods and received 15 cents per bag, with an additional five cents if the pods were dried. Every two bags of floss I collected would fill one life jacket. The U.S. military called for the collection of two million pounds of floss nationally, enough to fill 1.2 million life jackets.

I worked hard for my uncles and collected seven bags, the most of anyone in the school. I earned a total of $1.10. When paid, I bought a Bit-O-Honey candy bar for ten cents and gave the dollar back to the teacher to pay other collectors.

In addition to teaching us about milkweeds, the teacher was a specialist in many areas of curriculum. Each day she would call each grade level to the front of the room for recitation. On Friday we had spelling test and if we spelled all the words correctly, she put a gold star after our name on a chart hanging on the wall. I had gold stars for every week the entire year, and the teacher gave me a book written by Zane Grey as a prize.

When I was in the fourth grade, our teacher was a weak disciplinarian. One day the older kids made up a story and asked her to check something in the woodshed, the building out back where the coal and kindling for the stove were stored. When she went inside, one of them snuck out, shut the door, and placed a board in the latch so it couldn't be opened from the inside. Like everyone else, I sat in the schoolhouse for the remainder of the day as if nothing had happened, enjoying the luxury of not having to recite or study. At the end of the day, one of the older girls, Rosemary Knutson, felt remorseful, stayed after everyone left, and removed the board, freeing the teacher. With eyes filled with tears, the teacher told Rosemary, "I am going to report this to the superintendent of schools. He'll deal with the students who locked me in here."

The next day right after school started, the County Superintendent of Schools arrived at the door. The teacher got sympathy, and we sat very quiet during a stern lecture and threat of expulsion if we ever did that again.

I often listened as the teacher sat with eight different groups each day. I realized that the lessons she covered with these groups would be questions in the round robin on Friday. Students from the sixth through eighth grade would stand in the front of the school as Miss Sullivan would ask questions like "How many feet in a mile?" or "What is the name of the capitol city in Iowa?" If the students could not answer the question, they had to sit down. Because I had listened in on the lessons, I survived as the only one standing most of the time when I reached the sixth and seventh grades.

The school enrollees were a cross section of the Asbury population whose lifestyles differed from the cocoon in which I grew up. David and Mary Ann Batton traded comic books with me and taught me the facts of life when Mary Ann had her first period. Among the older students were two Herndons: Victor was studious; Vincent a bully. Vincent was always pushing and badgering me until I challenged him. He was less a bully after that. The Knutsons, whose homelife I described in *"My Hometown,"* used school as a refuge from their parents.

The front of the room was populated by the younger kids. Regrettably, I mortified Katie Oldham when I told everyone the story about her going potty in her seat. Another younger student, Delmar Minot, a Protestant who attended Church next door to the school, invited me and my brother to his house one Friday when we had a half day of school. Not realizing that as a Catholic we did not eat meat on Friday, his mother served chicken sandwiches. Not wanting to be impolite but not wanting to eat meat, I spoke for myself and brother saying, "We usually only have a glass of milk for lunch." Even though his mother suspected I was lying, she brought us each a large glass of milk.

There were two outdoor toilets, one for the girls and one for the boys. Each privy was a two holer, one seat higher and the other, lower for the little ones. I tried not to go to the bathroom during the winter as it was always freezing. If I just had to go, I raised my hand showing one or two fingers expressing my need to the teacher. She only allowed one student at a time to leave the room.

The outdoor privy was the learning area for a new experiment. When I was in the seventh grade, I was as tall as the older boys. I liked to imitate them to gain favor. Buddy showed me how to roll my own cigarettes. He stashed a bag of tobacco and cigarette paper for my use in the privy wall. During recess he taught me how to roll the cigarettes, light them, and inhale.

A typical outdoor toilet at rural schools

As a seventh grader, trying to act very grown up and discreet, I used my "privy" time to smoke. One day the teacher saw the cloud of smoke I blew out when I took too big a drag. When I returned to my seat, she came over and coyly asked, "How was the smoke?" Although I wasn't shocked enough at that, her next move was the kicker. She assigned me to write, "I will not carry matches or cigarettes on school property nor smoke them during the school day" 5000 times during recesses. The older kids in school had a good laugh at my expense. I was more careful in school in the future.

The smoking incident in the Fall of 1948 accelerated my passage through puberty, and possibly though junior high. I went through a lot of pencils and recesses for two cigarettes! More importantly, I was humiliated by my father's response. When informed by the teacher of my new" addiction," he decreed: "I will give each of my sons $100 if they don't smoke before they reach 21." My ego was tweaked a bit;

no recess for a year, and then I was deprived of the $100. I would have to find another way to come up with money to buy cigarettes if I smoked after I was 21.

At recess time in the fall and spring we would either swing or play ball. The swing set was very tall, tempting us to make our swing strokes higher than the top bar and then jumping off to see who jumped the farthest. We did all kinds of tricks on the slide—backwards, on our sides, headfirst—there was no limit to our creativity. In my last year's softball games, two older kids and I decided on a batting challenge to make the "little kids" stay out in the field. We tried to see how many recesses we could continue to bat without making an out. I guess that is why some of the younger players never really learned how to bat.

Occasionally we played hide and seek, but that became boring as the places to hide were few and obvious, so we'd turn to tag. I disliked it because the older guys could run the fastest, and again the younger kids suffered because they almost always ended up "it."

The teacher held parties on Valentine's Day, Halloween, and Christmas. We made Valentines with several colors of construction paper and decorated them with crayons. We gave Valentines to anyone we liked. I always made special hearts for Mary Ann Batton and Snap Ernster. They were in my grade and I wanted them to help me in class recitations.

It was always interesting to see who got the most Valentines (an early popularity contest). I was disappointed coming close several times but never winning.

When my brother Don was in fourth grade, he joined all who wore costumes for the Halloween party. Dressed as a girl wearing high heels, he was the last one standing. After we had guessed all the other ghosts and goblins. I had to admit even I didn't recognize him.

Christmas involved an exchange of gifts, and it was intriguing to guess what was inside the carefully wrapped packages. Most of the time I didn't know who drew my name until I opened the gift. I would try to sneak a peek under the school Christmas tree. The teacher caught me peeking and I had to wait like all the others. That was the end of my effort.

In need of big seventh graders, the teacher chose me and Ronnie Kifer to go find, cut, and bring back a Christmas tree for the school.

We left at the beginning of the school day. Using our American Flyer sleds, Ronnie and I found a tree right away and used an ax to cut it down.

Because it was still early in the day, I took my sled and went to a steep hill in the road that I had always dreamed about sliding down. Ronnie had decided to wait in the field with the tree for me. After climbing to the top, I set my American Flyer in front of me, ran a few steps to start, and began flying down the hill. As I came to the first turn, I looked ahead and saw a car in the distance coming toward me. I frantically steered to the side of the road safely sliding into the ditch.

My sled came to a thud, stopping under a couple of shrubby trees. I looked back and saw the driver of the car walking along the road, searching the ditch, and mumbling, "I thought I saw something go by me." I lay very still. I think I was still in shock but hoping he would not see me, as he was a friend of my family. Eventually he gave up and I heard the car start and leave the scene. I climbed out of the ditch, unhurt. When I joined Ronnie, still standing in disbelief at what happened, I warned him not to dare utter a word about what he had witnessed. Ronnie kept his promise and didn't tell anyone about my little episode.

Everyone was happy with the tree when we brought it in from the sled later that morning. We told everyone we had a real hard time finding the right sized tree and hauling it back to school. The teacher gave a knowing smile when she heard my story.

CHAPTER 22

A Change of Plans

In April 1949, my role at Asbury School took a sudden turn. Father Long, the parish priest, was concerned that the smoking incident could be the first domino to fall in my path leading to reform school.

Superintendent Flynn knocked on the school's door to meet with Miss Sullivan. Little did I know they were discussing me. After a bit they summoned me to come and meet with them. I shook in my shoes—Wow, did my smoking in the privy mean I would be expelled?

I was relieved when the conversation took an unexpected direction. Father Long had contacted the County Superintendent of Schools and arranged for me to take the eighth-grade examinations to qualify for high school. That meant I would be skipping from seventh grade to ninth grade in a new school. Suddenly my life was upended.

The superintendent instructed me to take the eighth-grade test in May, qualifying me to enter high school in the fall. Reality hit me quickly when my teacher said I had to study Civics and American History to prepare for the exam. It was already April. I didn't have time to be excited or worried about the test, let alone realize that I wouldn't be an eighth grader at Asbury School in the fall. A change of plans—for sure!

During my days at Asbury School, I had dressed as a farm boy. I wore shirts either made from flour sacks, or occasionally a store-bought shirt and bib overalls. My coats and jackets were hand-me-downs from Dad's youngest brother, Uncle Eldon. In winter I wore long john underwear with a button flap in back. My new shoes and boots were "ordered by mail" from the Sears and Roebuck catalog. Generally, I wore the same pair of shoes until I needed a larger size. The next year at Loras Academy would introduce me to a whole new world and line of clothing.

Bur clothing wasn't my only concern. I had to learn about American History and civics in the next few weeks. Some days I felt like I would never be ready to take the exams. But I felt encouraged when the teacher quizzed me at the end of the day the next few weeks and told me I was doing well.

When I went to take the test, I was still living in a world of anxiety, trying to get through this step. I sat down in a room full of kids who also were nervous. When I looked at the first two questions, the weeks of worrying left me. I had studied the right things! A month later I received a letter form the Superintendent's office notifying me that I had passed the tests and was eligible to enter ninth grade. I was so excited, I dropped the letter when handing it to Mom.

My parents agreed it was a good idea for me to move on before I got into more trouble. I think they were concerned about my future rides from home to school each day. School bus transportation for students didn't exist where I lived. They would have to either drive me to school or find other parents to share the commute. But they never talked about it. I think underneath it all, they were proud of me.

I finished Asbury School a month after I celebrated my twelfth birthday. I was sad leaving behind my two classmates of seven years, and especially other students with whom I had formed friendships. Mixed in that wistfulness was also an excitement to begin high school in the fall of 1949.

CHAPTER 23

A Twelve-Year-old Iowa Farm Boy's Winter Mornings before School

It's hard to introduce yourself to a cold winter day at 6 A.M. I heard my father's footsteps as he walked from the bedroom to the kitchen. I knew I had a few minutes to bury my head under the heavy quilt as he stood before the picture of the Sacred Heart to say his morning prayers.

And then the call came. Time to do the chores. I relished a couple more minutes under the covers before he came upstairs to make sure I was up.

In the dark before dawn I went looking for my overalls. The wood placed in the furnace the night before had burned up, leaving the upstairs bedrooms cold. Each morning my father added wood, stoked the furnace using a poker to stir up the coals, and warmed the house again.

I checked my long john underwear to make sure I had buttoned the back flap. Quickly, I slipped into my work shirt and bib overalls. Then I pulled up the long woolen socks and sat for a time, thinking about the coldly piercing wind that would soon be smacking my face when I went outside.

With no intention of hurrying, I went downstairs thinking about the day before me. I opened the woodshed door to the unheated area attached to the kitchen. I found my coat, cap and gloves hanging on the wall. Although cold, the room did not come close to the temperature I would experience when I stepped outside.

I put on my snow pants, slipping the elastic bottoms over my socks. Next came the coat with the hood, my cap and finally the boots. My gloves were frozen stiff; I had forgotten to put them on the furnace register to dry the night before. Their stiffness made them feel warm, but they were glacially cold.

My father had already gone to the barn. I walked crunch by crunch through the frozen snow, through the garden gate and down the path we had shoveled towards the barn. The walk was not too bad, but two waves of blowing snow still nearly blinded me as I approached the barn. I rushed to the door, opened it and was greeted by the warmth inside.

Although it was a cold, windy, winter day outside, the cows, horses, and calves were like a giant furnace, warming the interior of the barn. Often during the cold of winter, my brothers and I took refuge in the barn.

Now to work. I had to finish my routine chores, eat breakfast and dress for school before 7:30 A.M. First, I went to the horse barn to greet our two horses, Dick and King. I carried over my stool, curry comb, and brush and went to work. Their necks, heads and backs were taller than I was. I had to stand on a stool to accomplish my tasks. Using the curry comb, I first brushed the hairy coat on each horse's back and legs to make him look smooth and ready to be harnessed.

Harnessing a horse was a real challenge for me. The first step was hanging a large collar around his neck. The collar weighed about ten pounds. The top would spread open; my challenge was to lift the

Note how well I harnassed Dick and King

collar up around the horse's neck, pull a strap through a belt buckle and fasten it. The collar was important because horses push the collar to pull the wagon behind them. As they walk, this collar around their necks is attached to leather straps called tugs. The tugs extend beyond the horses and are attached to the wagon.

After fastening the collar, I went to the harness rack, lifted off the harness and placed it over the back of King. This was an especially arduous task as the harness was made up of Hames, wooden and metal links attached to large leather straps, all weighing about 30-40 pounds. And I only weighed 160.

The front of the harness had two Hames with brass tops. The Hames were wooden or steel curved shafts, fitting snugly into each side of the collar. The two Hames were held together at the top by a strap. They were fastened in place by a tug strap at the bottom of the collar. I was always happy the strap was at the bottom because I was not tall enough, even with the stool, to reach the one on top.

The brass tops of the Hanes were decorative. My father took great pride in those brass tops. It was my job to polish them and make sure they were always shining. My reward was having Dad say, "You did a good job shining those brass tops."

Next, I adjusted the harness over King's back. This included putting the crupper under the tail to keep the harness from sliding.

Horses sleep standing up and don't move much during the night. Some mornings my lifting the tail was the first stimulation, and I was greeted with a blast of the digestive system's work of the night before. Like usual, I tried to attach the crupper from the side of the horse to avoid morning fumigation.

When King was all dressed up for his day's work, it was Dick's turn. To ensure our friendship after dressing the horses for work, a last gesture was to go to the front of their stalls and check my handiwork. Although horses really don't speak, I often felt they would nod their heads saying, "Well done, Jim." Those imaginary nods made me feel they were my special horses.

One other chore remained before breakfast. The pigs were now stirring and hungry. I gathered two five-gallon buckets and carried swill to pour into the pigs' troughs. Our swill was a gourmet combination of water, skim milk and ground oats and poured like a thick soup. On cold mornings, the swill was not only heavy, but the snow was slippery in places. I had to be careful not to fall and be the first to sample the swill.

The pigs came out of their quarters into the cold air blanketed in steam. When sleeping they gather in a big pile to stay warm. I believe that is where the expression "pig pile" originated. They were a messy, grunting parade coming out to eat.

I threw ears of corn onto the feeding area we had previously shoveled free of snow, and then poured the swill into a long feeding trough. The pigs pushed one another to get a place at the trough, shoved their snouts in and drank. Slurping their chops, they wandered off to eat the corn on the cob.

Having finished my chores, I rushed to the house and changed into my school clothes. When gym class was not scheduled, I slipped into my long johns with the flap on back. On the days I had gym class I wore a special pair of long johns. My school clothes were a long-sleeved shirt, dress pants, woolen socks and school shoes. On cold days I wore snow pants and a hefty winter coat.

After dressing I dashed downstairs to eat. My favorite breakfast was a bowl of Wheaties or fried eggs and a scrumptious piece of Mom's homemade bread and blackberry jam.

Then I gathered my books and got ready for my ride to school. Since there were no school buses, my father and two other parents had developed a carpool on alternating weeks to drive me and neighbor kids to high schools in town. The parent who drove delivered us before eight in the morning.

And that's how it was. A twelve-year-old boy doing his typical winter chores on an Iowa farm before catching a ride to my freshman classes. I considered that daily ritual a normal part of my life. I did feel special though, having moved beyond my Asbury School classmates. I was now going to Loras Academy.

Chapter 24

Loras Academy

As a twelve-year-old neophyte in the hallowed halls of high school, I squeezed past the bulky football linemen, clustered conversationalists blocking the hallway, and derrieres protruding as books were removed from the lower levels of lockers.

Hesitantly, I found the half locker assigned to me, number 112. I opened the door, hung up my coat, and heard the warning bell for first class. I grabbed my texts and a notebook. Following the mass of bodies ahead of me, I reached the spiraling stairs leading to the next floor. Stomping feet led the way up a level to the second floor. The pace suddenly hastened as we scattered in different directions to classrooms.

Along the corridor, I noticed several of the students turning their heads and giving me a strange stare. When I walked into the classroom, one of my classmates chided, "Where did you get that shirt?" It was a combination of blue polka dot sleeves, a solid blue chest and back, and a striped collar. Mom's sense of Asbury style was obviously not in synch with that of teenage boys at Loras Academy. They bought their shirts at Roshek's store for boys and men.

Hour by hour the zingers about my shirt kept coming. In the break before my last class, I went into the restroom, intent on flushing the shirt down the toilet. Just then Dave Saunders, a classmate who had befriended me, came in, walked directly over to me and said, "That's really a neat shirt. All those guys talking like that are just jealous." Hearing Dave's comments, I felt less embarrassed and put the shirt back on. The shirt survived the day and so did the plumbing system.

That night I asked my mother to get me some store-bought shirts for the next week of school. She never asked why, and I did not explain. There were times growing up that I didn't have to explain my feelings to Mom. She just knew; this was one of those occasions.

Having survived the previous day's style test, I settled my gangly self into the desk and placed my books on its arm, focusing on the upcoming Latin class. Several times during the summer when I found out one of my courses was Latin, I had asked myself, "What am I going to do in Latin class when I have trouble writing in English?" The question hit me again. But now I didn't have time to wonder. Father Vogl began speaking and it would have to wait until later for an answer.

In class we were 30 students crunched together, and everyone was my age---so different than Asbury. I didn't know any of these guys, although a couple of them had said hello when I came into the room.

The claustrophobia of the locker corridor, the shirt remarks, and now all these unknown faces had me worried. Was this the right choice? What was ahead? Loras Academy was not only a Catholic college prep school; it was also a military academy. In my sophomore year, I would wear an army uniform and be responsible for my own M1 rifle. I would later care for a rifle and polish it like I had polished the brass nobs on the horses' harnesses just this morning. For now, I had to forget these drifting thoughts and return to listening to the teacher introduce us to a new language.

I was just a freshman and very happy not to have to worry about the military yet. I wouldn't wear a uniform and march this year. I just had to survive gym class and Latin.

Graduates of six elementary parish schools in the city comprised most of the student body. Those who were resident students, nicknamed boarders, mostly came from Chicago. Their presence created an atmosphere of "a reform school" for kids who were out of control at home and whose parents could afford to send them away to school.

As a freshman I was also introduced to the world of football. Loras Academy was a football powerhouse. The "Gubs" ran roughshod over all the opponents. Five members of the team were selected on the all-state teams and recruited as top college prospects.

The sports writers who selected the best teams in the state never fully accepted our school's schedule or invincibility. In my algebra class after our opening prayer, "Bump" Wagner, the assistant coach and teacher, would fill us in daily on the prejudice of the current slate of the sports writers. He was convinced they didn't like Catholic schools and would never rate our team number one. He believed there was no doubt we were the best team in the state.

He was befuddled by the sports writers and I was equally flummoxed by his algebra class. How does x=y + 1? I just didn't get it. The x,y puzzle followed me through the first quarter. When report cards came out, I had all 90s except for that inscrutable algebra.

Mom decided she would do something about my ineptness in math. Ruthie Ahrendt, the daughter of our good friends Bill and Rose, taught algebra in the public school. Mom recruited Ruthie, and her tutoring lengthened my school day into three nights a week. The first few meetings were tough, but she patiently helped me learn equations, and I began to look forward to showing her how proficient I had become in solving problems.

Ruthie really helped me remove the mental boulder blocking the x factor. I realized you could make x equal anything. Suddenly "I got it!" Although math remained a shadowy area in my learning, I did okay in algebra the rest of the year.

Four courses and gym/study hall composed my freshman schedule. Gym was two days a week; I had study hall the other three days. I grew to like gym. It reminded me of the games we played at Asbury School.

In the fall and spring, we met outdoors playing softball and other games. In the winter, we played basketball and volleyball in the gymnasium. Van Combs, the head basketball coach and gym instructor, used our class period to select and coach his future basketball players. When he threw out a ball after I was assigned to a team, I wasn't sure what to do. We had no basketball courts at Asbury School, and I had never played the game. Gradually, I learned how to dribble and shoot.

Later in the winter, my team advanced to the final round in our gym class tournament. When we came to the last seconds of the championship game, the score was tied, and I stood with the ball. Everyone on my team went silent. I had no choice; I took the shot. It went in. They couldn't believe it. They had never even seen me shoot the ball before. My teammates never passed the ball to me to shoot it. I couldn't believe it. I was like one of those little kids in the softball games in Asbury whom I never gave a chance to bat.

I proudly strutted to the shower room, shuttling among my tongue-tied classmates. A hot shower proved to be the best part of that gym class, maybe second only to my personal excitement and surprise that I made that basket.

Study hall was a warehouse of 100 desks, lined up in symmetrical rows front to rear. The desks were huge, comparable to half a kitchen table at home. Some of the desks had carved memorials of previous occupants either on the seat or the top surface. One day as I was diligently inscribing "Freiburger" as my memorial, the study hall proctor noticed my intense effort and came over. He said simply, "An etching of that size should be on a tombstone!" He handed me a piece of sandpaper and said, "Go to work. We already have your name recorded several times in our records." The proctor was the Principal, and I felt I had just dug my grave. I was concerned he would call my parents aside the next week when they came for Parent's Night. I feared this might be the high school incident rivaling my previous smoking incident. Fortunately, the etching was not mentioned.

My teachers at Loras Academy were dedicated and generally good. They were a mix of priests, lay men, and women. Most of the math teachers were women. Mrs. Lenihan was older and sometimes too fixated on the intrigue of geometry to notice the activities in the room. Intent on meticulously writing her theorems and proofs, she dismounted the platform and went to the blackboard, her back to the room. She unwittingly invited mischief of a roomful of semi-focused teenaged boys.

John Ahern was a case in point. A dedicated and perpetual class disrupter, John unnerved Mrs. Lenihan with his many antics. One day, completely frustrated, she blurted out, "John, I am going down to get the principal to deal with you." John responded, "If you go to the principal's office, I am going to jump out the window." The geometry classroom was located on the corner of the main building. Two stories below, attached to the same wall as the classroom, was a wide, flat garage roof.

Ignoring his threat, she stomped out of the room. John went over, opened the window, and slid down the rain spout to the garage roof. He sprawled out as if he had fallen and lay unconscious.

When Mrs. Lenihan returned to the room and announced that the principal was on his way, we were all standing at the window, staring down at the garage roof. She came to the window, peered down and saw John sprawled on the roof. She fainted. In the ensuing confusion, all attention turned to Mrs. Lenihan lying on the floor while John deftly climbed back through the window almost unscathed. When Mrs. Lenihan revived and sat up, she almost fainted again at the sight of John. The principal quickly sized up the situation, told us to take our seats and escorted John outside the room.

Later John told me that the principal took him by the collar and warned him in no uncertain terms: "If you ever pull such a shenanigan again, your stay at this school will be very short-term!"

Over the years I asked John why he had pulled those pranks when he knew he would get caught?

"School gets boring and I just wanted to liven things up!" Even though I didn't always agree with his antics, I have to admit he did add some excitement to our day. He was one of a kind and we remained good friends.

Mrs. Lenihan wasn't the only target of our antics. My history professor had a habit of describing an historical event by pacing in the front of the room, developing the historical scene, and then abruptly stopping and pursing his lips before saying, "etc. etc. etc." When he gave a quiz, the class decided to mimic his "etc." by writing an opening paragraph followed by "etc. etc. etc." He got the final "etc," though: "You are all getting an F, etc. etc. etc."

My favorite religion teacher had a quote when someone in the class was out of order: "Verbum Sapientia Sat," "A Word to the Wise is Sufficient." At the fiftieth reunion of my graduating class, I repeated his saying to him. He responded, "Did it serve you well?"

I replied, "Yes." As a teacher I used it several times.

Chapter 25

Kite Dreams

Is there a special magic inherent in kite flying? Does following a kite on its creative journey, searching for air currents above an Iowa farm, lead to dreams of the future? Does a young boy's future spin out like the lengthening kite string to reach new heights and adventures? Mine did, and many came true.

As farm life goes, nothing really exciting happened during my thirteenth summer. I was thankful for daily routine because other areas and seasons of my life were full. One area of my life emerged as eventful. My father was having a difficult time keeping pace with my changing attitude. The smoking incident in seventh grade had been a real setback in our relationship. Every time I got a little feisty, he would remind me of my depravity. Because I was now experiencing some degree of success in high school, I reminded him that I was doing all right for a 13-year old. Unfortunately, we had two different understandings of how well I was doing. My past smoking incident remained a major obstacle for me and my father to reconcile.

I was in another arena. I saw myself as that great person who was skipping eighth grade, going to high school and fantasizing my future. To soothe my ego and just enjoy quiet moments, I took up kite flying for the next year or two. I would find my favorite pine tree stump and happily sit and dream. Soon those dreams took form. Each dream was realized at a later stage in my future.

The first dream had come in the fall of 1949 during my freshman year in high school when I discovered football. A preoccupation with football had flooded my school, and 1949 was also a banner year for the University of Notre Dame. One of four undefeated college football teams in the country, Notre Dame was the overwhelming choice as number one. I would steal away to the barn and listen Saturday to the radio broadcasts. When I flew my kite, I dreamed of going to Notre Dame, mostly to watch the football games on Saturday.

Another kite dream took shape from the summer/fall farm events also that summer. Remembering those beautiful calendar pictures of Dad produced by the John Deere photographer, I thought back to other pictures displayed on each month's page, scenes from all over America. I was riveted by pictures taken in New England. Somehow those sunlit snow scenes with skiers were more appealing than the nasty blowing Iowa snow I had to shovel.

A third dream unfolded as I slowly unrolled the long string, launching my kite to dance in the sky. The stretch of string between the kite and me as well as thoughts nurtured by the many books I was reading, pictures, and the radio, carried me away to a city on a bay, San Francisco. To this day, though, I cannot fathom why I thought of San Francisco. All I knew was I had discovered that city and wanted to travel there. Once I got focused, as the string played out in my hand, I dreamed of crossing the mountains to visit this city far away on the west coast.

During the routine chores of the summer I struggled relating to my father, the worst clash happening accidentally. I lackadaisically drove the tractor into a ditch, and it got stuck. My father ordered me off the tractor and told Tom to get on while he hitched the horses to pull the tractor out. I was so angry that he replaced me with Tom that I stalked off, ran into the woods and pouted the rest of the afternoon.

Fortunately, kite flying and dreaming helped me through a long summer and gave me a sliver of hope for the future. I didn't realize it, but I had begun sketching the next stage of my odyssey.

CHAPTER 26

A New Stage

When I turned fourteen and had just finished my sophomore year in high school, Dad decided my younger brothers Tom and Don could do my farm chores. I was hired out as a farm hand to Philip Hoffmann. My parents saw this as an opportunity for me to earn money to pay my tuition at a private high school. I knew the Hoffmanns. Not knowing what to expect, I reluctantly agreed.

I worked at the Hoffmans Mondays through Saturdays. On Sundays I went to Mass with them and then spent the remainder of the day and evening with my parents and family. I was still an Altar Boy. Before Mass I had several conversations with Father Long about my life and hired hand experience. I told him I thought all my work at the Hoffmanns was old-fashioned and hard. He reminded me, "Your father is a progressive farmer; he is open to new ideas." As the summer wore on, I thought about those conversations and began to appreciate my Dad more.

Later in the summer, I experienced a harder way to harvest oats than my father's. Hoffmann cut the oats with a binder. The binder tied the oats into bundles and dropped them in the field. My job was "shocking" the bundles. I'd gather four bundles and stand them in a shock with the oats' kernels on top.

The first day while putting a shock together, I thought a lot about my father. Dad used a combine, which replaced the binder, shocking, and threshing machine. The combine cut and threshed the oats in one step.

It was a hot day. I removed my straw hat and looked at the shock of oats. Wiping my brow, I realized my father had adopted a better method of harvesting oats. He really was an advanced and efficient farmer. Why couldn't I have seen this when I belligerently disagreed with the way he did things at home?

Dad combining oats, 1951

Then I smiled, recalling harvesting oats at home the previous summer. When we had shoveled the oats into the granary, we had startled the mice families living there. While the oats were food for the animals we raised on the farm, field mice found the abundant food supply and made the granary their residence.

Dad considered them unwanted guests. He loved cats, and they all had names, some more colorful, like "Carbaldie," than others. He organized a cat invasion to disrupt the mice kingdom.

Gertie, my favorite cat, a three-legged-great grandmother who had met one of the machines on the farm and escaped minus a leg, was a star "mouser." I remember her squatting with one mouse under each of her two front feet and one in her mouth. I had a good laugh. I felt a bit nostalgic for home, especially picturing my father cheering the cats. I picked up the next bundle, checking to see if there was a mouse under it.

CHAPTER 27

My Curfew

On the farm, I drove the tractor so learning to drive a car was an easy next step. I passed my driver's exam on my fifteenth birthday. Dad bought a used 1939 Pontiac car. The timing was great. I had just finished my junior year in high school. Now I could drive Tom, who was beginning his freshman year in high school, and myself to school. He and I wouldn't have to traipse up the lane each morning to catch a ride.

The Pontiac became my car. During the summer I drove to my jobs, a toy tractor manufacturing company in the daytime and scoring softball games in the evenings.

The softball games usually ended around 8 P.M. and I joined my friend Rocky Schiltz to play tennis or hang-out at Eagle Point Park. After the tennis matches we stopped by the drive in for ice cream and I'd arrive home at midnight.

My Dad wasn't a fan of my being out late, He was having a hard time with my high school ambitions and behavior.

"As long as I'm head of this house, I will set the rules. I want you home by 10 P.M.," he ordered. Although I had grown to appreciate his modern farming, I didn't appreciate his strict parental oversight.

"It's my car and I'm perfectly able to handle my own life." End of conversation!

The night after he set the curfew, I met Rocky as usual. We played tennis and went to the drive in. It was after midnight when I arrived home. To further express my belligerence, I slept in the car. It wasn't easy, the seat did not slide back far enough, and I had to slouch over the steering wheel.

The next morning, I heard the garage door open and there was Dad looking in the car window at me. To my surprise, he didn't yell at me, but instead told me I had better go and apologize to my mother who hadn't slept all night. I sullenly ate breakfast, Mom said, "I have had enough. You can't keep rebelling against your father. I am going to call Monsignor Schulte and have him talk to you about respecting your father."

When Father Long retired, Monsignor Schulte had become the temporary pastor at our parish. Father Long told Mom, "Jim is interested in science and should talk to Monsignor Schulte. He teaches chemistry at Loras College and works well with students."

Mom called Monsignor and he came to the farm. She called me in to sit and talk with him. I respected Father Long, and because he said I should talk with Monsignor Schulte I agreed to the visit.

After asking a lot of questions he said, "You are causing your parents a lot of heartache. They don't understand why you are acting like this. Will you promise me that you will apologize to your father for staying out late that night after he asked you not to?"

I had told Monsignor I felt that Dad didn't like me anymore after I decided to go to high school and not become a farmer like him. He even hired me out to another farmer last summer. When he set that 10 P.M. curfew, that was the last straw for me. I did say that I was sorry I worried my mother.

"Your father and you should sit down and have a good talk." I was stunned. After telling my story, I thought he would say Dad was being too strict with me.

"I am still mad about the curfew, but I'll think about apologizing and try to have a talk with him."

I heard Mom thank Monsignor as he was leaving and tell him she would talk to my father. It was the first of several times that Monsignor Schulte would play a key role in my life.

I came home early the next night after I scored the games. When I walked in the house before 10 P.M., Dad said, "I'm happy to see you came home to sleep in your bed tonight."

"That car seat wasn't very comfortable." When I saw him smile, I knew we were starting over. We had taken the first of many steps towards rebuilding our relationship.

CHAPTER 28

Cutting Wood, Discovering Values

After the curfew incident, I was pleasantly surprised when my father asked me to help him cut down a tree. The saw had very large teeth, was about five feet long, and had a handle at each end. As we pulled the saw back and forth, the teeth engaged with the wood of the tree. Eventually, after many strokes, the saw would cut across the trunk and fell the tree.

Still hanging on to my all-knowing approach, I not only pulled the handle, but leaned on it to make the saw cut deeper with each stroke. My father called out, "Don't ride the saw." I shouted back, "Riding the saw makes it cut faster!" I was on the verge of provoking Dad again.

Suddenly, it dawned on me. I was working with my father and this was not school. Was I right to insist on riding the saw? Could my father have talked to me about using the saw before we began? For the first time I realized I might be setting the stage for another curfew-like incident. He stopped the sawing, reacting to the tone of my voice, and walked over to me.

I thought, "Here we go again." Dad also recognized the moment and made the first overture. He looked at me, smiled a bit, and then began to talk. I had a change of heart and chose to listen. He said, "I cut lots of wood when I was your age, and I, also had to learn not to ride the saw. It will do its work when you simply pull it freely."

Of course, he could have continued to let me ride the saw and suffered through the extra exhausting effort it required to fell the tree, or he could have called one of my other brothers who was more amenable to his method of sawing. But I quickly recognized he was right. Felling the tree was much easier if I didn't ride the saw. We went back to the business of felling the tree.

I learned how to use a crosscut saw. He shared his experience and gave me enough time to express my point of view. If he had chosen to assert his authority or if I had stubbornly refused to listen, we would have continued our summer feuding never having the satisfaction of felling the tree together.

The more I thought about that experience, the more I realized it was much more than a lesson in tree felling. Sometimes when I interacted with others, I was so caught up in my perspective that I didn't hear what they were saying. Once, when I was trying to tighten a bolt, my brother Tom came over and asked, "Can I help?" I gave a feisty, "No, I can do it myself," in response. He walked away muttering, "Jeez, I just wanted to help." We were both talking about the same bolt; I just had no time for Tom's point of view. Now reflecting on my past conflicts with Dad, I knew I had failed to take the time to understand him and the values he stood for.

Values remind me of a diamond. The diamond's value is determined in part by the number of facets it possesses. They are not one-dimensional and unbending rules. They are the source of many varied relationships with others. I began to understand that my values guide me to reach out and relate to others and hear the other person's point of view. When I thought back to Dad's and my relationship, I saw we had moved toward hearing each other's viewpoints. It reminded me I had to look at all the facets of a diamond before determining its worth.

Many years later I asked two of my grandsons to help me cut up some limbs in our backyard. I had a saw like the one my father and I had pulled. I told them the story of my father and me cutting down the tree. The boys and I had a "values summit" before they began pulling the saw. They commented afterwards it was great way to use the saw, but it would have been much easier with a chain saw. Dad would have had a good laugh if he had heard me tell them that I thought they were right.

CHAPTER 29

Upper Class Years

In the last three years of high school, I was a far cry from the uncomfortable, polka-dotted-blue shirt-of-many-stripes kid I had been. I felt proud the first day I put on my army uniform, and I soon emerged as a confidante and leader among my classmates. Several sought academic help and shared problems with me, and I developed true friendships.

I learned to march, fire a gun accurately, and care for my personally assigned M1 rifle. The ROTC program was referred to as "The Corps" and was led by a major and several sargeant instructors. Our courses, conducted three days a week, consisted of instruction in marksmanship, map-reading, first aid, leadership, and marching drills.

Weekly inspections of both my rifle and military attire were conducted. If the rifle was not cleaned, I was given "gigs," demerits that could result in afterschool punishment. I had two brass buttons on my military "Ike" jacket. I shined them weekly, the way I took care of the brass on Dick and King's harness. My rifle went "gig less" and my brass shone brightly.

In my junior year I joined the Grenadiers, a select synchronized marching group. We wore white helmets, white cravats, white chaps, and white waistbands. Our specialty was synchronized marching with ten others, performing "round-about-right shoulder arms" with our ten-pound M1 rifles.

Promoted to the rank of first

As a 15-year-old in my grenadier outfit with cousins Lyle and Wayne Wilgenbush, 1952

lieutenant in my senior year, I commanded the platoon selected as the best marching unit on our annual ROTC field day. After Major Martin pinned *The Chicago Tribune* medal for highest grade average and overall performance as a senior cadet on my chest, I looked out in the stands and saw my parents clapping. I drifted back in time to when I had stood cheering for Dad when he won plowing awards. Seeing Dad and Mom applaud gave me a real sense of pride and feeling of success.

During my junior and senior years, I engaged in several extra-curricular activities, serving as one of the editors on *The Crest*, the student newspaper. As a varsity member of the debate squad, I debated the role of the UN and the rights of nations in world governance. On the yearbook staff, I served as sales manager and staff writer. My 115 classmates cited me for two qualities: most reliable member of the class and the top Latin scholar. These honors culminated my high school years. But those freshman algebra grades created a distinction I could not have imagined as a freshman and affected my overall average and class rank. I graduated fifth in my class with a 94.5 average.

I had met with Monsignor Schulte several times during my senior year to talk about science and my future studies. Having decided on pre-med, I wrote Father Long and told him my decision. He wrote back, "You should plan on pre-medics and so let it be known."

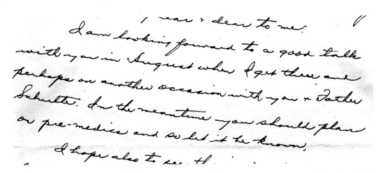

Father Long's Letter Giving Me Permission to Pursue Pre-Med - 1953

I was surprised because he had told my parents he thought I would become a priest. With this letter of approval, I could now look forward to my high school graduation and college.

CHAPTER 30

Loras College Years

Here I was standing in line to register for my classes as a freshman at Loras College, the big brother school to Loras Academy and a threshold to yet another new world. I had signed up for biology and chemistry, my pre-med requirements, along with three other freshman courses. The registrar acknowledged it, signed and returned the card saying, "Welcome to your freshman year at Loras." I felt both excited and nostalgic. I had a sense of adventure, wondering about my new classes and professors. Would it be like high school? Could I tackle courses that were new areas of learning for me? Would I survive the year as a pre-med student?

Then a bit of nostalgia set in. My best friend for the past four years, Rocky Schiltz, was going to the University of Iowa. We had spent a lot of time studying Latin, practicing baseball, and talking about our future college days. We had promised to write to one another during our first year in college. I looked around, hoping there might be another Rocky among these unfamiliar faces. Lost in thought I walked to the bookstore to buy my textbooks. Where was I in my life? I had moved beyond my Asbury farm years. My father was now warming to my desire to pursue a career as a doctor. He would ask, "How is life for the college kid?" He also told me several times, "If you need help paying your tuition, let me know."

I became more introspective in college.Thinking about how I'd changed from Asbury days, I could see a pattern. When I wore the ROTC uniform in high school, my classmates had seen me in a different light than when I wore that mismatched patterned shirt as a freshman. But it wasn't just the clothes. They had accepted me as a leader. Now in my science courses, I was learning not to accept things solely on face value, but to question, gain understanding, and draw my own conclusions. I realized that I had grown in other areas of my life but was still following the same Asbury catechism rules that had guided my boyhood. In discussing these concerns with a friend, I began asking questions about my religious practices.

One day while checking the school events bulletin board outside the bookstore, I saw a posting by Father Cyril Reilly "Anyone interested in joining a Young Christian Students (YCS) group, contact me." I met with Father Reilly and he explained, "YCS was adopted and translated to American college campuses from the Young Christian Workers movement in Europe." He wanted to start a similar group on our campus to educate students about the social doctrine and teachings of the Catholic Church.

He asked if I would be willing to form a group and meet weekly using YCS's action steps, Observe, Judge, and Act as a method of applying Christian principles. Hearing his description of YCS, I immediately thought, this sounds like what I am looking for. I volunteered to recruit others to form a group.

Searching for a way to build a better sense of community on campus, my YCS group developed a Big Brother Program for incoming freshmen. Working with the registrar, we gathered the names of the newly accepted 400 freshmen and grouped them by majors. We interviewed upperclassmen, using the guiding principle of "love you neighbor (in this case freshman student) as yourself" while serving as the Big Brother mentors.

I mentored a pre-med freshman and tutored him in chemistry. Our relationship grew as he shared homesickness and a roommate problem with me. At the end of the year, he met with me and said, "In the middle of my first term I was going to drop chemistry. Thanks to you my final grade is an A-." He continued successfully to pursue his pre-med studies.

YCS also led me beyond the church rituals of my youth to understanding the teachings from which those rituals had developed. As I began to grow in a new understanding of my faith, I wanted to encourage others in their own search to make church teachings and practices more meaningful. I began asking myself, "How can I assist others in their understanding of Catholic practices?"

CHAPTER 31

A Detour

Little did I anticipate what events would occur during my senior year at Loras College. I had carefully scripted the first three years of study, pursuing a pre-med curriculum crammed with science courses and a few electives. Now anxiety about the courses to get into medical school became my overriding concern.

I was looking forward to working as a counselor at Camp Foley for my final summer before senior year. I had friendships with counselors from the previous summer, including Jim Stessman and Jim Brady. Brady entertained us with his antics and stories many nights in the counselor's lounge.

Later he joined the staff of President Reagan as a presidential assistant and the fifteenth White House Press Secretary. He became famous, and disabled, when he shielded the President from an assassin's bullets. He and his wife founded a well known national movement on gun control. Congress, based on their advocacy, passed the Brady Handgun Violence Prevention Act in 1994.

But I wanted to return to the camp for another reason. The previous summer, on my first night off, I had met Carol, the waterfront director of our nearby sister camp. She became my first true love. On the remaining nights off that summer, we closed a lodge and bar on Trout Lake near her camp, singing "Teddy Bear Picnic" with the pianist. She had a great sense of humor, and I felt comfortable sharing my plans and dreams of the future with her.

Her parents came to visit during the camp season. After meeting them, I felt welcomed. Our relationship deepened. In late August after the camp season closed, she returned to her position as a teacher in Kansas City and I returned for my senior year, filled with expectations about my courses and getting accepted into med school. Writing and calling Carol added an exciting new dimension to my life.

The first week of school, Father Nye, the biology department chair and my advisor, called me to his office to tell me the med schools were cutting back on their admissions in the Fall of 1957. They were more carefully scrutinizing applicants to reduce the dropout rate. Suddenly, my stomach churned, and my anxiety peaked. Had my previous three years of study provided enough background for acceptance?

I applied to three medical schools. After posting the applications, I endured weeks of sleepless nights, waiting for their response. At last the first letter arrived, a rejection! The unexpected quickness of that response launched a black cloud on my horizon. A few days later, the second letter arrived, an acceptance pending an interview at Creighton University. I was excited. They asked me to go to Omaha the following Friday to meet with the admissions committee.

I boarded the Thursday evening train across the State of Iowa trying to sleep. All I did, though, was toss and turn, rehearsing answers to the interviewers: Why did I want to be a doctor? Why did I choose Creighton? What area of medicine was I interested in?

Arriving in Omaha a couple of hours before the interview, I washed my face at the train depot, stared into the mirror, and attempted to look alert and hide the restlessness of the train ride and the emotional roller coaster of the previous night. I felt very comfortable with the interview until one of the three interviewing doctors asked me to place my hands on the table. I cautiously raised them, concerned my hands were too large to consider surgery. Curious why they wanted to see my hands, I later discovered they were checking to see if I was nervous and chewed my fingernails.

When the interview ended, the three committee members thanked me for coming and assured me they would notify me of their decision within a week. I felt relieved for a few moments, but that feeling escaped me quickly leaving the room. I was remembering that first rejection and the black cloud returned.

Suddenly a thought popped into my mind. I realized I had been so focused on med school that I hadn't thought of an alternative. Maybe I should start thinking about it. Then, recalling the interview, I felt it had gone well and I decided to wait about alternatives until I received the committee's response. I regained my composure but was now exhausted and emotionally spent. I bought lunch and boarded the train back to Dubuque. The train seat became my bed, and the conductor, tapping my shoulder as we approached Dubuque, was the only conscious moment I had the whole ride home.

The third letter was waiting for me. The University of Iowa had accepted me as an alternate. Now I had an interesting dilemma. Do I say yes if I receive an official acceptance to Creighton, or do I wait for my personal first choice, Iowa, to invite me before I decide? Father Nye advised me, "Given the limited number of acceptances, if you are accepted by Creighton, I would make that your choice."

The promised response by Creighton arrived the next Friday. It was a letter of acceptance. I wrote two letters. In the first I thanked Dean Gillick, Dean of the Medical School, for the interview and for supporting my candidacy. The second was easier to write; "Yes, I would be happy to join the incoming class at Creighton in Fall, 1958."

Excited about my good fortune, I immediately purchased a microscope. Both my parents, especially my mother, were excited and spread the news to everyone. I wrote Carol that life was wonderful. I asked how she felt about being part of a med school student's life? She replied, "It sounds great to me. But I hope you will leave the lab and come home for dinner."

CHAPTER 32

A Fork in the Road

Each January the college scheduled an annual retreat for the entire student body. We gathered in the college chapel for talks by a retreat master and then spent the remaining time reading, reflecting, and doing rituals such as the stations of the cross. The retreat was timely for me. Senior year was passing quickly, and I needed some time to reflect on my future as a med student and I also wanted to think about Carol.

At the beginning of the retreat, I reflected on my past. I had an interest in science that was rooted in my mother's story and the lesson about potatoes. I had also enjoyed her nurse's stories about working with Dr. Plankers in the operating room. No doubt those stories influenced me in pursuing medicine as a career. Looking back, though, I kept hearing an echoing question: "Why didn't I study for the priesthood?" In the solitude of the retreat, I wondered why, suddenly, this question was reappearing. After all, the idea of studying for the priesthood had been settled when I received Father Long's letter.

Until this retreat, I had focused on the lofty goal of becoming a doctor. As a 12-year-old, blue-shirted farm boy, I had moved on from the farm to battling algebra and achieving that goal. I thrived on the academic competition required for acceptance into med school. Now, having achieved that, here I was in the quiet setting of a retreat, and the question raised by my YCS experience popped up again. "What role does religion play in my life?"

YCS had helped me see that the Church was about more than a collection of rituals. YCS, coupled with my parents' dedication to religious practices, stoked a seminal drive in me: How can I best learn and share the Church's teachings with others? What a quandary—becoming a doctor, marrying, having a family, and healing others? OR following my youthful aspiration to join the priesthood as a celibate guiding other in their experiences? I spent a sleepless night praying for an answer.

Totally obsessed with the idea, I made an appointment with the retreat master on day two. When we met, I attempted to share how bewildered I felt that, at this point, I would be asking this question. I muttered incoherently, but he nodded and said, "Are you coming to ask me to help you make your decision?" I sat silently considering his question and heard him say: "I think you have made your decision. Remember, God called Samuel three times before he accepted. St Paul needed to get knocked off his horse before he answered the call. Now I suggest you spend the rest of the retreat praying for guidance and expressing a sense of gratitude if this is your calling."

My whole being responded to his words and I said, "I know what I must do." I left his office feeling an enormous sense of relief, and I began planning how to tell everyone about my decision. I even considered which friend might buy my microscope. All I can say is that it was a liberating moment for me. It seemed my whole previous life, from the religious practices on the farm to my involvement in YCS, had led me to this moment. But how would I explain it to my parents, Carol, and siblings?

The retreat ended Friday afternoon. My parents were grocery shopping, and I asked them to pick me up on their way home. I walked to the corner of Loras Boulevard rehearsing how I would announce my change of plans. When they arrived, I didn't even warm the back seat before blurting out: "I changed my mind. I'm not going to med school. During the retreat I decided to go to the seminary." Mom's eyes filled with tears and she said softly, "Father Long always said you would be a priest." Dad drove home without saying a word. It had taken four years for him to accept my going to med school; this new turn in my life took minutes. He deeply respected the priesthood. He held Father Long in high regard. His silence was approval.

In fact, this was an epic moment for Dad and me. He was finally able to see me in a role making my own decisions. His ready acceptance meant we had moved beyond my past behavior and his pain of seeing me go in a different direction with my life.

Telling Carol was another emotional, challenging matter. It would have been so much easier if we could have sat and talked together as we had done several times. I had to grapple with the reality that, as a priest I could not marry. How do you tell someone you love that the only way the church will accept you as a priest is if you don't marry her?

When I was eight years old, my mother had helped me understand that humans have a special role on the farm, choosing the seeds and animals they will raise and care for. As I grew older, I saw Father Long as pastor of our church help my parents and others in the community celebrate rituals guiding them in their role as proprietors of their farms. The Church required that he not marry as a pre-requisite to serve in that role. Now I had chosen the priesthood and my choice required a commitment to celibacy.

In the 1950s Catholics accepted the fact that priests didn't marry. Carol might understand I had a "higher calling," but what about love and our relationship? Could she still accept this disruption? decision? —And could I?

The next few months we exchanged phone calls and letters; she agreed with my decision. We both resigned ourselves to the church discipline of celibacy. Carol best expressed our feelings when she said, "We have both grown because of our friendship. We can move forward, thankful our paths crossed." My first response was, Wow, she let me off easy. Then I wrote her a long letter thanking her and expressing my appreciation for her support.

Although my change of plans appeared to be radical, career-wise, it really wasn't. Everyone close to me was not really surprised by my decision or its abruptness. I was the only one that was shocked. I began taking care of some housekeeping tasks. How would I handle my med school status? I conferred with my advisor, Father Nye, and he advised that I write a letter to Creighton informing them I would not be enrolling. He suggested waiting until the end of the school year to ensure both of my decisions were firmed up. I mailed the letter in early May.

My final academic endeavor was writing the senior thesis. In partnership with three other classmates, we did an ecological study of the pond area on my parents' farm. Mr. Emmet Polder, my ecology professor, helped me with the research and writing, and gave final approval to my thesis.

Professor Polder was an ecological genius and what we refer to today as a "birder." When he came to work each day, he wore a heavy coat, boots, a rain hat, and carried an umbrella in spite of being weighed down by all his rain prevention paraphernalia, he had a bouncy stride as he walked along the sidewalk. Stopping to observe him, we would chuckle and say, "Polder bear is here to teach today."

On a field study with my class to our farm, he whistled bird calls. Within a 15-minute period he was communicating with meadowlarks, cardinals, song sparrows, and at least three other species. When Professor Polder saw Dad's dedication to soil conservation, he suggested that I do my thesis on that topic.

Months later, with the completed thesis in hand, I sat with my father and reviewed the maps and tests of the soil and water I had recorded. Page by page we reviewed the final document. He quietly and proudly commented about the charts and diagrams I had compiled. When we finished, I realized that I had presented his legacy—a document describing the farming practices to which he was so dedicated.

I could sense that he, even though I had moved on, growing up on the farm was an essential part of my life.

"I like your study. Now I realize that you haven't left your roots behind." Dad had become my hero when I looked at his pictures on a calendar. Now he was seeing himself and the farm through the lens of my life as his oldest son. My thesis completed and approved, I was ready to put on my cap and gown and cross the stage as an Honors graduate of Loras College.

Loras College Commencement
Don, Dad, Me, Mom, Tom – June, 1957

When I began my journey studying for the priesthood, one of my boyhood dreams became another chapter in my odyssey. Father Nye, Chair of the Biology Department, approached me about pursuing a graduate degree in biology. He proposed that I take graduate courses in the summer in biology and study theology during the regular academic year.

If I followed this plan, I would get my doctorate in biology and teach at Loras College after ordination. I was given a choice of taking summer courses at a couple of universities. One of the graduate biology programs was at the University of Notre Dame. No longer was I sitting on a stump flying a kite. This was reality. Slowly my odyssey was progressing.

CHAPTER 33

Major Seminary and Ordination

September 1958 arrived quickly, and I turned a new page in the calendar of my life. Here I was entering four years of theology at Mount Saint Bernard Major Seminary. The seminary served the four dioceses of Iowa. The rector and other administrative staff were priests from the four dioceses. The Dominican Fathers served as the theological faculty.

The seminary was located a mere five miles from my home. Entering the building it eerily felt like I was stretching the silken cocoon of my parents' farm. Mom contributed to that sentiment. She purchased an aluminum laundry box, picked up my laundry weekly, and returned cleanly pressed clothes. Homemade cookies and other tasty morsels were tucked in the neatly folded clothing. I found out from the porter that when he answered the front door to receive the laundry, Mom used the conversational guise sbout gardening to subtly obtain an update on my progress.

While I was putting on my cassock for the first time, I pinched myself asking, "Is this real?" Then as if looking into a mirror, it struck me. I was taking another step through life. The blue shirt my mother had made when I entered high school symbolized the first passage out of the shelter of Asbury. The ROTC uniform represented three years of growth into leadership, shaping my future. Then I decided in college to completely change the course of my life. And now in this monastic-like setting, I was donning a cassock, yet another garb, taking on theological studies and daily discipline that would send me forth as a priest.

Religion and Science

In the spring of 1958, scientist Julian Huxley announced to the world: "There is no separate supernatural realm; all phenomena are part of one natural process of evolution."

Huxley, an internationally recognized evolutionary biologist, eugenicist, shook up theologians and churches with that atheistic proclamation. Followers of religion were torn about discrepancies between the scientific "world of fact" and the theology of "faith and biblical revelation." Huxley's denial of God would follow me while I studied biology in the summer of 1958 at Notre Dame and in my theological program in the fall at Mount Saint Bernard's.

After one of my microbiology classes that summer, the instructor, Father Doll, called me aside. He told me how happy he was to see me studying biology as a seminarian.

He was the first of many who gave deference to me when I entered the seminary. I had experienced the role of Father Long as a benevolent authority, advising me about my future. Since making my decision, I was beginning to experience the priesthood as a hallowed role. Wearing a Roman collar had a powerful influence on people.

The conversation began with his asking if I knew of Julian Huxley and his atheistic stand based on biological evolution? I responded that I knew of Huxley and his reputation as a proponent of evolution. I added that I had heard he was an atheist. "After you are ordained, people are going to put you on a pedestal and seek your advice. It is important that you are informed on the relationship between science and religion. Remember as scientific knowledge grows, people will scrutinize the role of religion in their personal lives. Make sure you are informed and answer their concerns."

I thanked him for his interest in me. "I am glad you brought up this topic. But I am a bit bewildered about dealing with the issue." He responded: "Just be aware as you pursue your studies in both fields, that reconciling science and theology is very important. The issue will follow you in the years ahead."

His conversation introduced me to the role of science as an area of attention in my seminary training. Nurturing souls involved an understanding of the world in which people worked and lived. How would the next four years of study and preparation deepen my understanding of how science and theology fit together? Studying biology in the summer and theology during the year, would help strike a healthy balance in my education.

Preparing to Wear the Roman Collar

The staff of Mount Saint Bernard Seminary would ground me for my role as a priest. Our rector, Monsignor Frederick Heles, was a meticulous, clerically clothed, mannequin-like figure. Stoic, distant, authoritative to the last detail, he spoke with a distinctive impediment. He modeled discipline and decorum for our future roles. My only personal contact with him came when I was summoned to his office or if I had to make a major request.

He installed a traffic light outside his office. If the light was green, you could knock and wait for him to invite you in. If the light was red, you had to patiently wait for the signal to change.

The Rector spoke with a lisp. To spoof his aloofness, and certainly a bit disrespectful, we lisped to one another and called him "Fweddy." We were all shocked into an embarrassed silence in one of his weekly lectures when he announced, "You know, I have a lisp when I speak."

The second in command, the Vice Rector (a mistitled role—he was not the rector of vice), was shy but very personable. I enjoyed his class, *"Duties of a Future Parish Priest."* He prepared us for the rubrics of offering Mass and providing the sacraments to the parishioners. I will always remember his takeaway line about meeting with parishioners: "Prepare to enjoy a cup of coffee and a little cookie." I quipped to a colleague, "I hope the cookies are homemade."

The spiritual director was short in stature and tall in personality. He became famous for the stock phrase in his weekly lectures: "Let's call a spade a spade." He brought humor to situations. He demonstrated it best as celebrant at Benediction. The cope vestment (cape like), designed for a tall person, blanketed his short and stocky frame. When descending the steps of the altar, he would extend the cope with both hands creating the appearance of a wind surfer. At the bottom of the steps he would turn and kneel. Then he would kick the bottom of the vestment into a billowing tent. In the pews, as one of the taller students, I enjoyed his antics; the shorter seminarians identified with his affront to oversized vestments. When he was celebrant, we referred to his entourage of candle bearers, master of ceremonies, sub deacon, and deacon as "the short people celebration."

The surname of the director of music was Lyon. He had a very prominent jaw; we referred to him as "the Lyon's Jaw!" For four years, following the same routine at lessons. I would sing the scale as he accompanied me on his piano. During the remaining minutes, I would do diaphragm and breathing exercises. Under his tutelage I advanced from being tone deaf to singing on key.

The speech director also met with me weekly. Early on he informed me that I was mispronouncing my "s." In the first year of my lessons, he had me place gum inside my lower teeth to train my tongue to rise so that I would blow my "s" through my upper teeth. My first thought was why hadn't someone told me in the past 20 years that I was saying z instead of "s" After a year of my gum and his persistence, I now blow my "s" in the upper chamber of my mouth. Correctly pronouncing "s" was one of the significant accomplishments of year one." Other topics covered in speech class were sermon preparation, lesson plans for classroom teaching, and proper proclamation of the scriptures to an audience. I had learned how to compose a speech, a skill that I sorely lacked until that time.

Every Saturday for four years my work assignment was with "Pops" Kuenzel in his sequestered Umberto Eco, "The Name of the Rose" library. Called out of retirement, he was charged with assembling and organizing the seminary's library collections. He spent the weekdays stenciling the library code numbers on the bindings of books. My work detail was placing his finished products on the shelves and then organizing the following week's work. Often, the other workers and I would gather around as he smoked his Kool cigarettes and gestured his palsied hands vigorously while telling a story. "Pops" was a genteel, grandfatherly mentor to me.

As a group in those four years, my seminary professors modeled and prepared me to wear my Roman collar responsibly as an authoritative representative of the Church.

Daily Discipline

A seminarian's whole day was orchestrated by bells. A bell in the morning woke us up, and an evening bell sent us to our rooms in silence. Years later, the discipline associated with the bells still occasionally rings in my head. I rose with the 6 A.M. bell and went to the chapel with everyone else for meditation and spiritual reading (sometimes nodding off to sleep) followed by Mass at 6:45 A.M. Some mornings before leaving the room, I thought of myself joining Dad in his ritual of praying to start the day.

Breakfast in silence followed Mass. Then we escaped outside, and the outdoor patio would explode with conversation, the first time we could talk since 8 P.M. the previous night. Many quickly lit and puffed on their first cigarette of the day because we could not smoke in our rooms. We had little or no media access to the outside world, so we colorfully entertained each other with dreams of the previous night. Most accounts got interrupted when the bell sent us rushing to our rooms to collect our books and go to class.

Learning the Teachings of the Church

The rituals I practiced when living on the farm had their derivation in the scriptures and church teachings. In the seminary, three classes covered the roots of our rituals in the Church's teachings from the early days to the present.

The *Summa Theologica* of Saint Thomas Aquinas was our major source and guide. Areas of study included development of the sacraments as sources of grace in our lives, the controversies about Jesus being both God and man, and whether we were predestined by God or were free to choose our own destiny. Other courses traced the Church back to the 12 apostles and defined the Pope's role of authority in the Church. Those four years of study prepared me to teach Church doctrine and to give meaning to the rituals I had practiced as a youth.

Our dogma instructor had a ritual of his own. Usually he taught at a desk on a large podium in the front of the room, he would occasionally step down and stand in front of the class to lead a discussion. Invariably when he attempted to go back to the podium, he would bounce his leg off the edge. His jousting with the podium happened every class, and I, along with others in the class, would quietly moan, feeling his pain in each of the repeated collisions.

In moral theology courses, we learned theories, guidelines and rules for a Christian life. These courses emphasized the laity and had a strong emphasis on sexual, medical, and workplace issues. The instructor turned every topic into a genealogy of commentators and their perspectives, ranging back to the 12 apostles. Although I am not a fan of trivia, I spent much of my time in his courses comparing the number of commentators on each topic. I was also fascinated with the way the Church adopted Pagan practices, like the anointing with oils, and included them in the sacraments, such as the blessings of babies in Baptism.

Our scripture studies traced Church teaching to both the Old and New Testaments. Both scripture professors were educated in the Holy Land and were well prepared to help us find our way interpreting and understanding the Bible. We nicknamed our New Testament professor "Pearl" because he often would say in class, "This verse is a pearl of great price."I got to know "Pearl" better when, in my fourth year of seminary, a Dominican bishop from Ecuador stayed on my parents' farm to learn about American agriculture. On the final day of his visit, the bishop and my Dad visited the Dominican Priority where my instructors resided. The bishop, of course, became the center of attention so Dad moved to the sideline to observe and wait.

"Pearl," who did not know my father, was confused about his role so he went over to my Dad, pointed his finger and asked: "You Ecuador?" Surprised by the question, my father came back with "No, Father; the bishop is staying at my farm and asked me to bring him here today. They both had a good laugh and a great conversation.

It so happened that my dogma instructor, who knew our family, had attended the reception and overheard the whole exchange. The following morning in class, the dogma instructor walked over to my seat, pointed his finger and asked: "You Ecuador?" Seeing my puzzled expression, he laughed and told me the whole story of "Pearl" and my father.

It was a gratifying experience for me. It took me back to my roots. The bishop's visit gave me a whole new recognition of the value of my parents' accomplishments and their way of raising me. I was proud that a bishop would stay at our farm and seek advice from my father. "Pearl" announced to the whole class at our next meeting that he had had a wonderful visit with Mr. Freiburger. My stature as a student flourished.

In more boring moments in class, we also dubbed our Old Testament professor, "Chum!" (Fishermen use bait called "chum" to lure fish for the catch.) As he presented the Old Testament stories and events, he would always, in a very alluring manner, align the happenings, people, and the cultural settings before a major inter-vention by a prophet or God in Jewish history. He was excellent in "chumming" us to grasp the significance of Old Testament events.

Silence

The discipline of silence was supposed to be observed in the living quarters, in the chapel and the main corridors, in other words, pretty much any place inside the building during the day and evening. I must confess to some "silent" whispers and gestures in those corridors. Silence demanded a self-discipline that I had not experienced.

As a group of resourceful seminarians, we found alternative ways to communicate—Call it clerical humor. Sometimes when walking in the corridor I would mime singing the scale as if I were in my voice class. One of my classmates told me even in silence I was not on key.

In my first year, I was surprised as I stood in line waiting to take my shower, when one of the deacons arrived dressed as the Pope and wearing a Tiara (Papal crown). The deacon accompanying him held a censor filled with smoking incense. He went down the line of bathrobed guys and blessed us with clouds of smoke. As the "Papist" left the room, he placed his finger on his lips shushing us to silence.

The spiritual examen of conscience also had an important role in the discipline of the seminary. We gathered in the chapel before lunch and the spiritual director would read aloud questions from the *Spiritual Exercises of St. Ignatius,* including questions for us to apply to our behavior and thoughts: Are you respectful of others? patient? Although the questions were intended to help us improve our own personal behavior and attitudes, more often than not, they made me feel discouraged about my spiritual progress. The examen raised other personal issues I was trying to deal with. One question I often considered was isolation from family and the events of the world. Right there in the seminary I was experiencing one of the effects of that isolation.

The fourth-year students, now deacons, did inject some levity into the somber tone and seriousness of the spiritual examen. Situated in the chapel sanctuary facing toward the middle of the nave, they looked out at the underclassmen in the pews. When the spiritual director would pose a question such as "Am I proud and vain?" one of the deacons would discreetly nod at underclassmen out in the pews. We in the pews would snicker if we agreed or disagreed with the deacon's assessment of others in our ranks. Despite, or maybe because of the added levity, I carried the practice of "Examen" into the rest of my life.

But levity had no place on the menu in the refectory. Every day I observed seven Franciscan nuns prepare and serve our meals from behind a metal pull-down curtain in the kitchen. The nuns were dedicated to culinary work in seminaries. Sequestered away, they had no contact with the seminarians or the world. At mealtime, they raised the iron curtain and food appeared in bowls and dishes. Underclassmen were assigned to serve the dishes for each table. I remember one little game when I was a server. To break down that wall of separation, I tried to peek into the serving window and make eye contact with the nuns. After a couple of tries, I could tell that word traveled quickly behind the barrier. My last attempt was met with a cold stare from a very stern nun. I walked away hoping being celibate wouldn't also make me humorless. I wondered if my isolation would influence the way I dealt with women and other people in the parish.

When one of the seminarians was assigned to read during the meal, we kept the rule of silence. I looked forward to those occasions when the rector would announce after the prayer before meals, "Gaudeamus! You may talk." With full voice, we'd respond "Deo Gratias," Thanks be to God. While the readings were mostly meaningful, we all enjoyed conversations at table. The mix of people at tables gave us a chance to talk with many whom I usually didn't see. I considered these meals the best part of the daily schedule. They brought back the storytelling around my own family dinner table. One of my best memories was being at table with Joao Ripoli from São Paulo, Brazil. His stories about growing up in a Favela, a poor neighborhood of wooden and cardboard shacks, were heartrending. His story took me back to all the kids my mother had helped. Table assignments were changed every month. Through these table rotations I developed many new friends. Many thought the rector's rationale for the new assignments was his concern that cliques would form if we always sat at the same table. Considering the alternative of four years at the same table, I agreed.

Two informal rules were part of the table rituals. First, the deacons received the food first. Second, when the serving dish was passed, if you did not take the dish, the person handing the dish dropped it on the table. I remember the first time I was the victim of a dropped dish. In the silence of the dining room, the sound of the dish hitting the table drew the stares of everyone.

After the meal we would recite "Ave Verum" and make a chapel visit. Following the visit, we went to our rooms for study or a siesta. The siesta ranked very high on my list. From my early days on the farm I always found early rising difficult, so I appreciated this mid-day nap, until yet another bell sent me off to afternoon classes.

Leisure Time

Following the afternoon classes, we had a recreation period, a time for playing sports, pursuing hobbies, or taking walks. I participated in several sports activities—touch football, basketball, softball and handball. I won several tournaments in this last sport. Most of all, I enjoyed the walks. The grounds had once been a racetrack and training area for trotter horses. The track encircled a large pond; the area surrounding the seminary was open countryside. Often, we would check the goldfish in the pond and explore other wildlife on walks.

On these walks I formed close friendships, giving me trusted fellow seminarians with whom I could share my concerns. Bob Couch from Davenport, Iowa, was one of my first walking companions. In his teens Bob was hospitalized with tuberculosis. Only after given a clean bill of health was he accepted to study for the priesthood.

During his illness, Bob was treated in the state hospital. His illness and the hospital's distance meant his family visited infrequently. When Bob chose to study for the priesthood, several sponsors volunteered to support him. One couple, Howard and Emily, lived near the hospital. She was a nurse and had cared for him during his illness. He spent his vacation periods and most of the summer months with them. I developed a friendship with them through Bob. After Christmas with my family, I spent part of the holidays visiting Bob at their house. Bob, Howard, Emily and I played cards, and we welcomed the new year during a card game, singing Auld Lang Syne several times.

Bob, like Rocky in my high school days, became a close friend. He was one of the most empathetic people I have known. He engaged in constant antics "to loosen me up!" One evening, after we returned from a vacation, I found a baby turtle with a water and feed bowl at my door. A note said, "You can call him Bobby. Remember he needs your love and attention daily." The turtle survived as my companion for a whole semester. Although the turtle's stay with me was a short one, Bob and my friendship extended for 18 years when he died of a heart attack.

On one occasion Bob invited me to Davenport to meet a special guest staying at Saint Ambrose College. While at breakfast, the guest, John Howard Griffin, joined us at table. John had traveled the South as a white man and then as a black man. He had just returned from his second journey recounted in his book, *Black Like Me*. Blotches of the black dye, injected to change his skin color were still evident in his arms. He described how demoralizing he felt when he had to drink at colored fountains and use black-only restrooms. His worst experience, when hungry one evening, was not being allowed to eat in the same restaurant he had eaten in as white man several months before.

While I heard him narrate his story, I recognized that the import of his venture into the world of prejudice and segregation was totally foreign to me. I was still comfortably ensconced in my little world at Mt. St. Bernard Seminary, learning all the good things I could do to save people. Bob was trying to help me expand my horizons.

Another seminarian and I had shared several experiences as counselors at Camp Foley and had been classmates at Loras College. Jim Stessman was a free spirit and progressive thinker. He was the editor of the college literary magazine and an avid reader. He tutored me when I wrote my first published story.

Jim and I had a friendship with Father Dolter who taught three of my chemistry courses. Although he appeared aloof and preoccupied to most of the students, Father Dolter singled me out and several times invited me to sit and talk about my studies and plans. Father was bald, and when he lectured, the light brightly reflected off his head. We students nicknamed him "chrome dome." Jim had volunteered to work with a Church camp in Brooklyn during summer break. When he met with Father Dolter, Jim found out he was driving to New York at the same time, so he hitched a ride hoping to learn about science and chemistry. Later Jim confided to me it was the longest two-sentence trip he had ever taken.

Our seminary curriculum focused on the writings of St. Thomas Aquinas, a thirteenth century theologian, and reflected medieval thought, especially regarding science. A movement called Modernism focused on science was emerging in the Church. Jim became interested in Modernism and wanted to start a study club on the movement. The idea was banned by the rector.

One morning when the buses arrived to take us to the local Cathedral for liturgical services, I boarded early to find Jim and another seminarian sitting in the back having a discussion. They hushed their conversation until they saw it was me. They were having an off-the-record conversation about science and Modernism. Suddenly I realized that I was one of a small group engaged with the issue of religion and science.

When the opportunity came, I took the role of the scientist in my discussions with Jim and a few other seminarians. Occasionally in my mind, I reverted to the lesson plan my mother had used to tell me about potato life. Science, as Mom had conveyed by her potato story, goes from factual knowledge to theory. The scientist gathers facts and comes to an understanding of how these facts fit together. Using this approach, the scientist learns from his data and integrates the information to explain the phenomena.This explanation is proposed as a theory. This method of learning emphasizes the role of the observer or learner, which contrasts with the teacher presenting the concepts and applications.

Finally, in my fourth year one of the younger instructors raised the issue of evolution and Julian Huxley's comments for discussion. Where does God fit into evolution? Using the scientific method Julian Huxley concluded God doesn't. We spent two class periods discussing the dilemma: Does science lead to atheism, or to belief in God? After those discussions I wondered if I would ever be able to bridge the chasm that I felt between teachings that came down through the ages and the findings of science in the contemporary world.

I often thought of Father Doll's advice that I should strive always to give people the correct information. My summer courses had introduced me to genetics and evolution. Again, my early learning on the farm served as a base. Dad's intuitive understanding of improving crops, was now backed up by science, showed that my Dad's methods made sense.

Special Times and Weekends

During my first year in the seminary, on the first Saturday of the month, I caught a taxi and visited my sister Margaret, a postulant in her convent. We both shared our feelings about our new life setting. I could write and receive mail (it was censored by the rector), but she could not. Much of our conversation would be catching up with our siblings. She would ask questions like, "I wonder how Tom likes his courses at Iowa City?" or "How do Mary Jo, Bill, and Mike like St. Anthony School?" We also talked about the games we had played as kids and just the freedom to go for a walk and sit under the shade of a tree. We were both happy about the change, but we agreed our lives were now more regimented and removed from the world around us.

Fortunately, I had occasion to share my farm experience growing up with fellow seminarians. Because my home was in the Dubuque area, I could invite others to join me twice a year on a home visit. I usually invited seminarians from distant places. Mom always had some goodies, and we would spend time visiting and exploring the farm. These were delightful episodes as my parents went all out to be good hosts.

Our Sunday schedule began at seven with meditation and Mass. The highlight of Sunday Mass was the homily delivered by one of the deacons. When I was a deacon, my turn came on the feast of Christ the King. I spent hours trying to compose my sermon around the verses in Matthew, where Pilate asks Jesus if he is a king. I'd spent several visits with the speech instructor reviewing my drafts. Both faculty and classmates complimented me afterwards. I felt relieved after working so hard on the content and delivery.

On the last Sunday of the month, family visitation time was 2-4 P.M. in one of the large classrooms. During the four years of study, my family faithfully attended each of those visits. Only later did I realize my brothers had arranged their visits back home from the University of Iowa just to sit quietly in a classroom for two hours on Sunday afternoon to visit me. I never felt I thanked them enough.

When the visit time was over, we went to chapel and chanted Vespers. My parents always looked forward to attending. We exited down the aisle past the guests when we finished. I tipped my biretta, a hat we wore to chapel liturgies, as I passed their pew hoping to catch my parents' eyes. They cast goodbye smiles back. While we were separated by seminary walls, this gesture symbolized the close ties that continued to grow over the four years.

On visiting Sundays, I went back to my room after Vespers to explore the gifts they brought me, either food or contraband, like a book. Dinner followed at 6 P.M. followed by silence and preparation for the week ahead.

My Ordination

I woke up early the morning of March 17, 1962, after a restless sleep. After visiting the chapel, I ate breakfast and quietly spent the morning pondering my ordination. It was an overwhelming realization that my preparation was complete and today I would become a priest.

The bus arrived and the 16 seminarians to be ordained went to the Bishop's Church, the Cathedral of St. Raphael. It had a stone exterior dating back to 1861. Although the interior of the church still contained much of its original decor and structure, the sanctuary and altar where I would kneel and pledge my obedience to the Bishop, were expanded and renovated.

Each year at the Easter vigil service, the Bishop blessed the chrism oil he would now use to anoint my right index finger and thumb representing the priest's role in consecrating bread and wine at Mass. The ceremony poignantly displayed that I would become a man set aside. My ordination climaxed four years of challenging study, discipline, and semi-isolation from my family and the world in preparation to my return to that world as an official representative of the church.

After the index finger and thumb were anointed with the oil of chrism, my right hand was wrapped in a cloth called the manutergium. A Holy Cross Sister whom I'd met the previous summer while studying at Notre Dame, specialized in making the cloths. She volunteered to design and paint biblical symbols of the priesthood on my manutergium.

In Church tradition the role of mother of a priest has always been held in high esteem. This esteem gave rise to a pious legend surrounding the manutergium:

In earlier days the tradition of the manutergium called for the newly ordained to present it to his mother. When she dies, her hands are wrapped with the cloth. When she arrives in heaven, she is escorted with her wrapped hands directly to Our Lord. Our Lord says to the woman, "I have given you life, what have you given to me?" She hands him the manutergium and responds, "I have given you my son as a priest. At this Jesus grants her entry into paradise." (Catholic Encyclopedia)

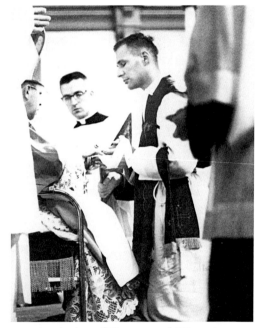

Anointing of Fingers and Wrapping with Manutergium

I had informed Mom that the real purpose for initiating the manutergium into the ceremony was preventing the chrism oil from staining the expensive vestments used at ordination. We gave due respect to the cloth, but when I told her of the legend, she smiled and said, "You should keep the cloth as a remembrance of your ordination."

Ordination was a mystical experience. As part of the ceremony, I lay face down on the sanctuary floor as the choir chanted the litany of the saints. It was overwhelming to hear the names of so many who were either priests or had been served by priests from the past. And now I was assuming this role to assist others to sainthood. During the ensuing weeks, I was astounded by the aura of my new role. My parents too, were amazed at the number of congratulatory comments they received.

My ordination was historic for two reasons: First, in the Catholic lineage of five generations in my family, I was the first priest. Second, I was the first ordained in the history of the Asbury parish where I grew up. Traditionally, everyone growing up in the community either returned to farming or factory work in nearby Dubuque.

As my ordination grew near, all my relatives had joined in preparing for the First Mass and reception. My grandfather offered to purchase my breviary, the book of prayers I would say each day as a priest. Several aunts and uncles contributed towards the fund to buy my personal chalice. Everyone became involved in celebrating the event.

The pastor engaged the entire parish community in preparation for my first Mass. It was held in the parish Church. Father Cyril Reilly, who had been chaplain and mentor in YCS while I was in college, delivered the homily. Father Warren Nye, instrumental in my going to Notre Dame and studying biology, was the deacon. Father Bob Couch, a close friend during my seminary years, was the subdeacon. The whole parish community was involved in the music, decorating the church and setting up the reception area in the school. I was overwhelmed when I walked down the aisle to exit the church after Mass was over.

Following the Mass, we had a luncheon and gathering for family and friends. Father Nye served as the master of ceremonies and toastmaster for this celebratory luncheon.

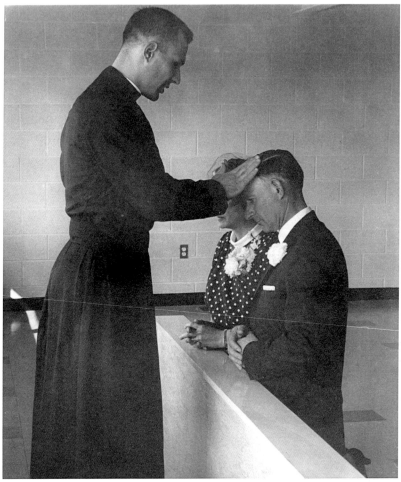

First blessing for my parents

Later in the day the parish school was opened to receive guests in the formal reception. My parents and family stood beside me in a receiving line. A kneeler was placed immediately in front of me. The guests knelt and received my blessing. The guests were very generous with their donations. The monetary gifts enabled me to buy a suit, clerical garb, and eventually a car. The reception had special meaning for my parents. Their oldest son was now a priest. After returning home that evening we looked over the attendance register. My parents shared the many compliments and comments they had heard. The funniest was my Aunt Anita saying, "Pope John XXIII was too old to be drinking martinis and running the church. Did I really want to work for him?"

The day after the celebration I returned to the seminary to complete the remainder of my studies. Upon completing the courses, I underwent an examination on my pastoral role. The success of four years of study hinged on this exam. It certified my legitimacy to function as a priest if I understood and applied the moral principles of the Church in the case posed by the examiner.

He posed a sample case I might hear from a penitent in the confessional. Nervous, I responded, hoping to demonstrate an understanding of the case presented and how I would guide the penitent.

The case posed for me involved theft. The penitent had stolen food from the grocery store. I asked the penitent how he would restore the stolen materials or make up for the cost of the food. After he responded with a solution, I sought his resolution not to steal again, and I assigned a penance for him to perform. The examiner agreed with my response. His response lifted the weight of the whole four years of study. After passing the exam, I was granted "faculties," a form of certification, to function as a priest. Finally, I requested a "Celebret," an authorization letter from my Bishop, permitting me to offer Mass and hear confessions in dioceses other than Dubuque.

Duly scrutinized and documented, I set out to launch my priestly duties. I now was a man set aside to carry on God's work assisting people in answering their questions and leading their lives. I felt relief that my four years of preparation were over. As I left the seminary behind, I was anxious to begin functioning in my new role. The next question was, where would my assignment take me? My parents hoped I would be located near them. I, too, hoped it would be close enough that I could visit them frequently.

I felt secure I had mastered the Church's teachings. But underneath I felt a little twinge of concern about that science/religion question and how I would deal with it in the future.

Chapter 34

Priesthood

In June after ordination, I attended summer school at the University of Notre Dame. Words cannot describe the adulation I received as a newly ordained in the presence of hundreds of nuns also taking courses. Every day included a request to offer Mass or bestow a first blessing. When one of the nuns expressed how wonderful it was to have a newly ordained priest in class with her, I had to step back and ask myself whether she was reverencing the priesthood or idolizing me.

I often chuckled when I thought of my experience the previous summer. I was anonymous as an aspiring student and seminarian. Now it appeared the Roman collar and the halo attributed to sainthood were one and the same. As the summer passed, I was still lost in the distinction. I enjoyed it but also realized it would be fleeting. And it was.

I left Notre Dame in August and abandoned the halo in South Bend. When reporting for my role as a parish priest, I rang the doorbell. A woman's voice called in the distance, "Come in." I did and found the housekeeper was lying on the living area sofa, her arms and legs wrapped in saran wrap. She was suffering from a severe case of psoriasis. Without a word of welcome, she said, "You're the new priest?"

"Yes, I am reporting for my assignment."

"Well then go upstairs, your room is on the right." Not a word about the pastor. I went to the car and carried my bags and books to the room.

A few hours later, I heard the pastor ask her whose car was parked outside. She said "The new assistant arrived a couple of hours ago. I think he is in his room."

"Good, I guess I should go up and see how he's doing." Such was the welcome to my first official duty. I no longer needed to worry about Roman collars being confused with halos.

In the rectory and parish, I was the last, and least in rank and status. The pastor devoted most of his time supervising the janitor on the grounds and maintaining the buildings. Each weekday during the school year, he celebrated the eight o'clock Mass for the school kids. Occasionally, he heard confessions and conducted a Friday Novena with a chosen number of parishioners.

He headed up the Priest's Blue Cross Health Plan and the Retirement Fund. Many late afternoons he spent in his office, sipping martinis and writing checks. These pre-prandial cocktails prompted stories during the evening meal with the other assistant, the housekeeper, and me. The pastor always led the conversation and set the tone. He was an inveterate fan of Jackie Gleason. As we ate dinner between hearing confessions every Saturday evening, Jackie's antics with Norton and Crazy Guggenheim, were rivals to his commentary on Jackie's life.

His favorite time was in the evening watching TV. I would join them after my evening appointments to review the day. Many a night he shared his disappointment about not being recognized and promoted to a higher level, becoming a bishop. I felt sorry for him. His ambition had turned bittersweet.

My Parish Role

Preaching and hearing confessions brought me closest to the parishioners. More than wanting to clarify and enforce rules, I strove to support the parishioner's efforts to be Christian. I tried to be open and friendly with everyone, attempting to remove the aura of one "set aside." But it was hard to let go of that preoccupation with rules.

During the first several months, I also focused on my sermons. Several brave souls took me aside and gently told me I was not looking at people when I preached. One dear lady, Lilly, said, "I want you to talk to me, not read to me." I was taken aback and gulped hard to swallow my pride. I had to shift from reading a lesson plan-type sermon to speaking to people from the heart. It took a while, and some awkward how-am-I-doing-stares from the pulpit, at my critics. Eventually, their guidance led me to personalize my sermons, and in doing so I found it easier to focus on the spirit of the beatitudes and speak less of obedience to rules and laws.

Sometime later, Lilly met me after one of my sermons and said, "I felt you really talked to me today, and that made it a good message." Thanks to Lilly, I learned how to preach on Sundays. Many of the parishioners over my three-year stay in the parish commented they liked my sermons. I always said, "Thanks to Lilly!" In the seminary I had learned how to compose a sermon; my parishioners had taught me how to deliver it.

Father Rethamel, the first assistant, was very conscientious and a devotee of the pastor. He arranged our daily schedules for offering Mass, Sunday baptisms of the newborn, and other weekly duties. He and I heard most of the confessions. We rotated hours in the confessional box. He usually started around 4 P.M. on Saturdays. I would relieve him at 5 P.M. and hear confessions until 6 P.M., dinnertime. We both returned to the confessional after dinner. I liked having both of us there, as it was a good time to read my daily breviary prayers or polish my sermon while waiting for penitents.

Confession can be a powerful experience. Making a good confession rids oneself of guilt and creates a sense of forgiveness. Unfortunately, more and more rules and practices about the sacrament had accrued through the ages, and it had often become merely a ritual.

Two practices impacted the role of confession in the lives of Catholics. First, the Church Fathers determined that at seven years of age, children had reached the age of reason and could commit sins. The seventh birthday initiated a lifelong practice of going to confession. Although it was very ritualized, I came to realize that, if handled sensitively and in an age appropriate way, Confession did raise awareness, even for seven-year-old children, of how our actions affect others.

Secondly, the lifelong practice of confessing could be a source of spiritual guidance and direction for many. For others, Confession had another meaning. The Church said that you had to go to Confession and Holy Communion at a minimum on Christmas and Easter to make your "Easter duty," or you could not receive Communion at Mass, be married in the Church, or have a Church funeral.

I had to deal with that rule on one occasion. I received a phone call that a non-church going father had a heart attack and died. I went to the home and gave him the last rites, anointing him with the holy oils and granting final absolution from his sins. He had died suddenly, and his wife was still in shock. I knew his daughter Cindy, who was active in the parish youth group I advised. That Sunday afternoon Cindy had gone with a group of kids to a restaurant to celebrate a birthday. Her mother asked me to pick up Cindy and share with her the most difficult news: that her father had died suddenly. I informed the group that Cindy's mother asked me to pick her up because something serious had happened. On the way to the car, I somehow broke the news that her father had died of a heart attack. She sobbed, and I placed my arm on her shoulder. She sat quietly and after a few moments of silence asked, "My Dad didn't go to church. Will he have a funeral Mass?"

I was able to say, "Yes." I had gone to her home when her father died and given him the Last Rites and would preside at his funeral Mass. I was determined to do so because I believed the Church's role at the time of death was to offer consolation and understanding, rather than judgment, to the family. It was one of the Church's Corporal Works of Mercy. I further felt the Church's role was to be a source of reconciliation for the deceased's family.

Hearing Confessions

I can still see the line of 30 second graders awaiting my arrival to hear their confessions. Looking at that line up, I thought to myself: It is amazing that seven-year-old children are labeled as sinners. As I approached, I could see Sister Angela gently moving each child to a position in the line. She alternated the boys with the girls to prevent nervous mischief.

I assumed my confessional seat, placed the violet stole over my shoulders and waited for the first footsteps. Slowly, the child first in line came and opened the door. A nervously breathing unseen form appeared at the window that was draped in a red sheeting. There was no sound. I quietly whispered the prompt, "Bless me father..." A half whisper responded, "for I have sinned. It has been one month since my last confession ...." Next followed a teacher-organized list of transgressions.

The most frequent, and I might add the most flagrant admission of guilt I heard from the line of petite penitents was "I disobeyed my parents." The second on the teacher's list was "I said bad words," often meaning I called my friend a name yesterday on the playground.

Then I would thank the deeply penitent child for coming to confession and seeking God's forgiveness. Continuing, I would say, "To show God you are truly sorry and will not disobey your parents in the future, say three Our Fathers or three Hail Marys as a penance." Next, I prompted them to say a sincere act of contrition. While they said the Act of Contrition. I raised my hand and made the sign of the cross "absolving them of all their sins."

After we both finished, I said, "You have made a good confession. Now go in peace."

With a sigh of relief, the child would open the door for the next child to enter. After sliding the door shut over the cloth window, I would open the other side. A nervous seven-year-old boy waited there to begin. Sister Angela had prepared the entire class very well. Only a couple kids froze in fear and needed special help from me.

The seventh and eighth grade classes had more worldly experiences when they came to confession. They approached more practiced in coming for the sacrament. They used cadence and whispers to camouflage serious transgressions. Many were truly contrite and relieved after they confessed. I tried to communicate a sense of forgiveness and understanding, reminding them of the importance of other people in their lives. Most of all I felt challenged to help them distinguish between sinning and being a bad person, reminding them we all make mistakes and can change.

Often two of us heard confessions in the same time period. My presence as a second confessor offered adults choice for their confession. Those who came to me ranged from individuals who delivered an unpunctuated list of transgressions through a hand shielding the mouth, to those who truly sought spiritual direction. One of the greatest challenges when hearing confessions of parents was trying not to reinforce their guilt about being angry with children, but rather helping them recognize what makes them angry so they could learn to deal with it by developing understanding and patience. Often, I felt at a loss, sitting isolated by a screen shielding me from the penitent. I felt anonymous and impersonal trying to hear someone's confidential and intimate confession of transgressions.

The Vatican Council, 1962-1965, addressed my concerns about Confession. The Council greatly improved the meaningfulness of the sacrament by changing the setting. In the early Church people confessed to the community and sought forgiveness. The ultimate expression of confession is reconciliation with those we have hurt, and ultimately with God. The Vatican Council shifted the setting from the priest sitting in the confessional to the choice of face to face to create a more meaningful exchange between the penitent and priest. I think of this new setting more as that of a doctor listening to a patient describe his or her feelings and symptoms before he makes a diagnosis and prescribes medicine. This approach to confession, along with the addition of silent acknowledgment of guilt at the beginning of Mass, were first steps toward changing the present form of Confession back to the early Church's practice of communal public penance.

Sunday Baptisms

One Sunday, it was my turn to baptize 16 babies. I returned to the rectory and remarked to the Pastor, "With all these births, we should discontinue the trains that run by parish neighborhoods, waking up people in the middle of the night." The pastor immediately replied: "That's your assignment: Follow up with the railroad." It became an ongoing joke at Sunday's baptisms.

Although cries of babies echoed through the church, parishioners at Mass complained about the inadequate sound system in the church. Father Rethamel announced the men's society wanted to donate money for new speakers and microphones. The pastor obliged and installed the new system in the church. As the celebrant at Mass, we now wore a portable microphone hung around the neck with a switchbox attached to the belt. The pastor was a bit befuddled and wanted to practice the first time he wore the microphone. He eventually attached everything but forgot to turn off the switch. He went into the bathroom adjoining the area where he was preparing for Mass. His bathroom visit, especially flushing the toilet, was broadcast to all in the church. For weeks, he was complimented on how well the new sound system worked.

One of the great privileges I had as a priest was to officiate at weddings, especially those of relatives: two of my brothers, Tom and his wife, Pat; Don and his wife, Eleanor. During my stay I was also privileged to preside at the wedding of three of my first cousins. It was a gratifying experience to share these joyful times in their lives.

My official assignment was at Holy Ghost parish, but I had a secondary assignment to teach at Wahlert High School. Although I didn't realize it at the time, that latter role would become my sole future assignment. My parish duties included offering Mass each day and on Sundays. I taught religious education classes to the public high school kids. I was chaplain to the Women's Rosary Society, director of the parish youth club, and athletic director for the elementary and junior high sports programs. I really enjoyed this last role and worked with some excellent coaches of the football, basketball, and track teams. The parents were pleased with my guidance. Several of the students were successful as they progressed through later academic and athletic careers. It was always rewarding to hear from them as the years went by.

One student, Terry Trieweller comes to mind. During Terry's high school years, I served as his confidant and mentor. He was a talented athlete and bright student. He went off to college, and our lives took different paths over the next 40 years.

During the writing of this memoir, I googled Terry's name. Each notation in his biography was impressive. I was not totally surprised even to find that he had served on the Supreme Court in the State of Montana. A video gave me a firsthand view of his acceptance of "The Trial Lawyer of the Year" award, earned for his role as one of the lead prosecutors in a $400,000,000 settlement by a Swiss pharmaceutical company. Novartis was charged with fraudulent kickbacks and aggressive sales tactics.

After watching the video, I called his office immediately and left a message. Several days passed without a return phone call. I assumed, so goes the glory of my tutelage. Understandably, I figured, those 40 years and Dubuque, Iowa, were a world away from Montana.

A few days later while working in the yard, my cell phone rang. "This is Terry Trieweller," the voice announced. He explained that he postponed the call because he, his wife and their three daughter and grandchildren were vacationing together. To my surprise, he said he wanted to share "the influence you had on my life during my high school years with them before I called." He told me he visits his mother in Dubuque and asked if we could meet there. After a long conversation we agreed to meet when I visited Iowa. It was then that he reminded me he must have seemed like a nuisance in class with all his questions. True, he was active in class: a quizzical look would appear on his face, and then the hand would go up. "Father, Could you explain..." I shared that it was a pleasure having him in class; he livened things up!

I met with him in Dubuque later. I admire his loyalty to his roots and his family. I was also reminded of the fact that, as teachers, we learn so much from our students. In this case, long after the classes were over, I was impressed the learning still goes on.

Parish experiences came in many variations when you consider that 1100 children of parishioners at all levels of income attended grades 1-8 in the parish school free of charge. One family living in poverty had several children in the school. The children were undernourished and poorly clothed. Sister Grace, one of their teachers asked me to visit their home. The rules in her Order of Nuns did not permit her to do this kind of work.

I discovered there were seven children, three months to 12 years. In addition to his regular work, the father set pins at the local bowling alley to gain extra income. In a subsequent visit I asked an accountant to sit with them to attempt a budget. Income even from the father's two jobs was insufficient. Tapping other resources, I was able to assist this family with clothing and food.

During one of my later visits, the question of having more children came up. Don and Joan were obviously faithful and devout Catholics parents. They were told in confession they could not practice birth control, a Church teaching seriously impacting their family. For the first time I was faced with the reality of their family poverty not resonating with the moral advice they were given. More children would have consequences for the future of the living seven and the welfare of this family. Before I left, I gave them the name of a doctor who could counsel them and told them I would contact him. Later I would help them set up an appointment. As I was leaving, I felt in a bind. I realized, as a representative of the Church, I could not in good conscience tell them to come to me to go to Confession. In my judgment, ensuring the welfare of the family, especially the future of the seven children, was more important than observing a medieval teaching about birth control and the role of sex in marriage.

After that conversation, I left this family realizing there was more to my role in the Church than enforcing laws. I had to assist people to make their own decisions. My responsibility was to help people to learn Christian principles so their conscience could be their guide and not just blindly follow rules issued by Church authorities. Saint John Henry Neuman in his Letter to the Duke of Norfolk expressed my feelings when he said, "I shall drink to the Pope, if you please, still, to Conscience first, and to the Pope afterwards."

This dilemma led me back to my questions about the role of religion and science. Father Doll's words echoed in my ears, "Make sure you give the right information when dealing with people." Reflecting on his advice, I felt secure that I had guided this family correctly to the best of my ability.

Marriage Counseling

Fortunately, an occasion arose during my second year in the parish, to reach out and assist parishioners in another manner. Carl Reilly of the county attorney's office contacted me to serve as a pastoral counselor in pending divorce cases. His office established a mandatory policy requiring couples petitioning for a divorce to seek counseling, preferably with a representative of their faith. I accepted the role as one of two Catholic counselors. The counseling service was publicized as available and free for anyone to meet with a representative of the religion of their choice.

When all the twenty counselors met, we discussed the question of access. The court referrals approach was working. We unanimously agreed that the service should be publicized and available to anyone who might seek counseling in earlier stages of marriage crisis. The co-director came up with a very creative approach. Bartenders have a sympathetic ear for people who cry in their beer. To assist bartenders in their empathetic role, we decided to invite them to a dinner and explain the referral process.

What an unusual gathering: Twenty clerics, including a Jewish Rabbi, milling with 100 bartenders, glancing quizzically around the room for a corner to hide.

To keep the bartenders engaged, we promptly invited them to be seated for dinner. After the grace before meals, Attorney Reilly removed the aura of mystery and explained why we had convened them. Quiet laughter filled the room and then all stood and applauded. A female bartender spoke up: "Wow, now I can put up a shingle saying, 'Come cry in my beer, and I'll help you find someone to solve your problem.'" The bartender strategy worked. Suddenly, the other counselors and I were getting phone calls for appointments referred by bartenders. Sometimes a creative idea coupled with a free meal yields results.

The birth control issue came to the fore in 1965 in a strange manner during my last year in the parish. One of the Vatican Council directives was changing the language of the Mass to English and turning the altar around to face the congregation. Impressing on the pastor the importance of educating the parishioners, I got his permission to recruit and prepare a group of laymen and women to initiate the changes. The music director of the seminary I attended volunteered to lead the education of this group.

At the end of each training session, several members of the group would stay and talk about the Council and its teachings. In one of these sessions, Lloyd Avenarius raised an issue about the Vatican Council, emphasizing that the laity should make decisions in their lives based on Christian principles, not just follow the rules. I could tell by his questions he wanted to pursue this topic further.

He called me the following week. He was a pharmaceutical representative and wanted to meet with me about a new product his company was promoting, the birth control pill. He began the conversation by explaining that the birth control pill was designed to control the ovulation period in a woman's cycle. "You told me the other evening the Vatican Council emphasized providing information to the laity, so they could make decisions based on their conscience. The Church teaches you can't practice birth control, but this pill can be used for that purpose. Will Catholic women be able to use the pill?"

After a bit of reflection, I realized the science of the pill made sense. "Your explanation has educated me. I realize it could help married couples in two ways: First, couples having trouble conceiving a child can use the pill to pinpoint the time when conception might occur. Secondly, for couples using rhythm, or abstinence, usage of the pill can help avoid an unwanted conception." He responded, "How about women who just use the pill to avoid pregnancy altogether?" We both paused, and nodding our heads, realized we had returned to the whole question of what criteria people use to make decisions.

If they followed the rules of the Church, the pill, a contraceptive, could not be used. But if the decision was based on personal judgment, then it was a whole different situation: the pill, depending on their intent, could be used for good or bad reasons.

I now had the other bookend of my dilemma with the family whom I had earlier advised to use birth control. It was not just a matter of following or not following the law of the Church; the decision to use birth control was anchored in each person's conscience, raising the question, why were they using the pill? Was I, as a priest, helping people form their conscience? It was a question I needed to resolve.

In August 1965, I was appointed as a full-time faculty member at Wahlert High School. While in the parish, I had taught religious studies classes at Wahlert. I enjoyed the teaching role and now I looked forward to doing it full-time.

My parish experiences had deepened my knowledge and understanding of people's day to day lives and the decisions they had to make. I also recognized more fully the science/theology dilemma. On my last Sunday, I said goodbye and thanked the parishioners for the opportunity to serve them. I packed my belongings and moved to a new assignment. It was August, 1965.

Chapter 35

Wahlert High School Faculty

My new assignment included living in a local landmark mansion. I was pleasantly surprised when I found Vianney House bordered a farm which, at the turn of the twentieth century, had bred world-famous trotter horses. I felt right at home with a farm next door, reminding me of my days harnessing horses. Unlike my modest farmhouse though, my new residence was a spacious living quarters on the first floor, a large sitting room and a bedroom. With some assistance I painted the walls a soft forest green. For the first time in my life, I was able to invite guests to join me in my personal quarters. It felt like old home week in a new home. Our family's door was always open to visitors. Now I had my own welcome mat.

I may have been a new faculty member, but I had life-long ties to two of the students: they were my two younger brothers, Bill and Mike. I never taught Bill, a junior, but during my first year I received daily reports on his activities from two of his teachers. I finally had to inform them I was his brother, not his parent, and I thought he was a good kid. I indicated that they should report their concerns to the Dean of Discipline. That ended their daily reports. I assumed Bill either reformed or kept his actions under their radar. Mike and his future wife, Diane, were students in the marriage course I taught in their senior year. Hopefully, the course has inspired them through 30 years of marriage.

When appointed to the faculty at Wahlert as a 28-year-old, I was the youngest priest who lived at Vianney House. The principal of the school, Father Larry Guter, was my former high school teacher. When I enrolled in the minor seminary, he was the rector, so we had often sat and reminisced about the many experiences we shared during ensuing years. The two of us had a memorable experience when he was my rector. The residence hall had a 10 P.M. lights-out curfew. I was reading an intriguing mystery and decided to finish it one evening after lights-out. To hide the lamp, I made a tent by stretching a blanket over my bed and head. To ensure I was safely hidden, I did a trial run while the rector went outside after the curfew hour and conducted his window inspection from the yard, checking for cheaters. I watched as he rounded the building past my window. He didn't pause. Assuming he saw no visible light, I proceeded with my plan.

Usually when he returned to his room after the inspection, he came up a stairway near my door. I'd then hear him walk in the hallway to his room. On this evening I decided to listen for his footsteps and then retire to my tent to finish the mystery. But first, another mystery.

I heard a door open, but there was no sound of steps in the hallway. Listening more intently, I didn't hear the door to his room close. Suspicious, now I got down on my knees and peered under the door. There he was looking back at me, both of us staring wide eyed at one another. Instinctively, I moved back and jumped into bed.

A few minutes passed and a folded note appeared under the door, "See me in my office after chapel in the morning." Groggy from lack of sleep and with great trepidation, I knocked on his office door the next morning. Almost immediately, I detected a sly smile forming as he began the conversation. He advised me, "Go to bed on time or I will have to campus you." (confine my existence to the dormitory). Ultimately, we both had a good laugh.

My closest colleague, Bill Franklin, obviously nicknamed Ben, was head of the guidance department at the school. I spent countless hours with him assisting students. We developed a close friendship that lasted through the years. Many experiences during my five years at Wahlert added to my personal growth. I shared my faculty office with Galen Thomas, a layman, the athletic director. He had been one of my own teachers during my high school days. He was a quiet man who seldom spoke about himself or his family. One day he turned to me and said, "I have never really talked about this with anyone. Martha and I had two sons. While at the beach one day, both boys swam out too far. I jumped in and could only save the youngest. I have lived with regret ever since. As the years passed, I devoted all my energy to John. When he was ordained a priest, I felt rewarded for saving him." I teared up. I was overwhelmed and all I could do was go over and put my hands on his shoulders. We had a long, profound moment of silence together. He was very proud of John, and he had every reason to be. I felt privileged that he trusted me enough to share his story. We had more conversations as time passed.

Galen's son, John, left the priesthood a couple of years later. With a choked voice, his father shared, "I saved John's life when he was drowning. Now it's time for me to step aside and allow him to pursue his own life." It was a powerful message. Galen had lost his oldest son. Now his second son was changing his path. I began to realize how my Dad must have felt when I changed course away from becoming a farmer.

As department chair of religious studies, my main duty was to supervise ten instructors and ensure the curriculum reflected the Church's teachings. Concurrently, the Second Vatican Council was meeting in Rome. Significant changes were taking place in practices and teachings of the Church. Many "canonized" saints were being removed from their pedestals, and among other changes, Catholics could now eat meat on Friday. Although the veneration of the saints was embedded in Catholic practices, I felt strongly it was important to return to the core of our religion, the death and resurrection of Jesus. Not eating meat on Friday as a Church regulation grew out of a medieval period enriching the Holy Roman Empire which was deeply invested in the fishing industry. I was happy the Church teachings and practices were returning to the gospel message.

One of my roles was working with the instructors in overhauling textbooks and teaching materials to reflect the new direction the Church was taking. We had to change from the past emphasis on rules and practices in textbooks to an approach focused on teaching the gospel message. I oversaw the revision of classroom instruction to reflect these changes.

Areas we had to deal with included teachings conflicting with the findings of astronomy and the Genesis story of creation; teaching biology, especially the functions of the human body and the findings of modern medicine which seemingly put us in conflict with the medieval beliefs embedded in Church laws. Once again, I was trying to resolve the conflictual status of religion and science. An opportunity to achieve this integration came unexpectedly. Father

Guter called me into his office. "We need a sex education program at Wahlert!" I couldn't believe my ears. I asked sarcastically, "Is this for the faculty or the parents?" He laughed, "They both need it, but I'm thinking of the students." So, that directive helped me implement one of my goals. Integrating religion and science at Wahlert High School began as an adventure.

Father Guter loved to experiment with the curriculum. We were already offering a marriage course for seniors taught by a team of two lay members and two priests. During the semester we had guest presentations on dating, courtship, and wedding planning. Married couples related their experiences with communication, spirituality, and finances. Many of the students expressed their appreciation for the course. Using the marriage course as our model, I assembled a group of teachers and parents to plan the new program. After several meetings, we chose the sophomore year for the sex education program. The biology teachers were responsible for the anatomy; two priests were selected to meet with the sophomore boys and two nuns to meet with the sophomore girls to discuss the moral issues. We decided to separate the genders at this age to create a more open atmosphere for questions and discussion. We launched the program, and there was great enthusiasm among the students. Just talking about sex is a motivator for kids this age. I was amazed at the range of questions: "Where do babies come from?" to "Do boys want sex more than girls?"

At the end of the term, we asked the students to give us feedback. Religion teachers asked the students about the anatomy or biology discussions. Biology teachers queried the morals segment and the discussions in the religion teachers' sessions. One suggestion that emerged was to show a movie about human anatomy as part of the biological discussions. The principal sent out an announcement and description of the sex education program in the newsletter for parent-teacher conferences. The names of the teachers and their teaching areas were included. The newsletter became the main agenda of the Catholic Mothers' Clubs. Each of the eight parishes in the City had a club. A representative of each club met monthly with a city-wide board. After several Wahlert mothers, who were members of the clubs, received the newsletter, our program became the buzz of the clubs, and the chair of the board requested a meeting with the principal and teachers involved with the program. The principal and I composed a letter, setting a date and the school library as a meeting place for club representatives. We restricted attendance to the members of the citywide board. We explained that parents attending parent-teacher conferences would have the opportunity to ask questions or express concerns before we met the Mothers' Club representatives. We hoped the conference responses would give us a clue whether the Mothers' Club supported or opposed the program,

After the parent-teacher conferences, I collected all the questions and concerns the parents expressed. I was pleased to see a positive response. I felt less nervous about meeting with the Mothers' Club reps who I at first feared as outsiders, would represent the traditional attitude, "We don't talk about sex publicly."

The night of the meeting arrived. The principal and the teachers who had been part of the program greeted the "Mothers' Group. Father Guter, welcomed everyone and introduced the teachers. I led off the presentations, explaining that we had a marriage course for seniors and described the course content. Using this course as a guide, we had brought together a planning group to develop the program and we chose the sophomore year as the best year to present it. Then the teachers described their roles in the program. At this point we opened the meeting for questions and discussion. The questions were mostly focused on the content of the program. We were able to emphasize the program and its content and not deal with such issues as teenage pregnancy or contraception. Then the president of the mothers' clubs rose, thanking us for inviting her and the club members and asked how we had come up with the need for a sex education program.

Father Guter answered, "As principal it is my job to identify curriculum needs for Wahlert's students. When I looked at our curriculum, I found there wasn't a real sex education program. I called in Father Freiburger and asked him to put a program together. I'm convinced he did a good job, and we got excellent feedback from the students who participated. We invited you tonight, even though our role is to work with the students and parents. We hope you think this is an important program and will take that message back to your club members."

The president waved her hand and stood up, speaking in a challenging tone of voice, "Father Guter, I respect your role as principal and the need for a good education for our children. The women here with me tonight are mothers and parents. We didn't come for a lecture. We came for information about the program, which Father Freiburger and the teachers explained very well. As they did so well tonight, may I request that Father Freiburger, and the other teachers, if they are available, come and explain this sex education program to our individual clubs. That is the best way I think we can support what these fine teachers have done. And may I further say, I think Father Freiburger is an excellent priest and teacher. I would like the members of my mothers' club to get to know him better." With that constructive statement the meeting ended. We lingered over soft drinks and cookies to answer any further questions the club representatives might have. I was greatly relieved. When I returned to our residence, I saw Father Guter's light was still on, so I knocked on his door.

"How much did you pay the Mothers' Club president to make her comment tonight?" I told him that she had come to confession a couple of days ago, and I wouldn't give her absolution until she praised me and the program at this meeting!

The sex education program was deemed a success by the team, students and parents. It reflected attempts by Vatican II to reconcile the differences between religion and science. Although I had a background in science and theology, I was further convinced I must become better informed. This realization led me to reconsider my summer school assignment.

CHAPTER 36

My Odyssey Takes Me West

During the summer months when the school was not in session, priests assigned to teach were sent to pursue degrees in administration and counseling to meet accreditation requirements. In March I received an assignment to pursue a degree in counseling. I was serving as "spiritual director" and head of the religious studies department at Wahlert. The assignment to study counseling surprised me. I really thought it would be more appropriate to pursue graduate work in religious studies. I thought back to an earlier decision by the Bishop which had disrupted the plan for me to pursue biological studies. I also realized that if assigned to pursue religious studies, I would be the first priest at the high school level assigned to pursue that area.

The religious studies program was the core of Wahlert's mission. The Vatican Council had addressed contemporary issues, and the program should reflect those teachings. While counseling was an important role, as department chair I needed to update my understanding of those teachings. I made an appointment to meet with the diocesan superintendent of schools to discuss changing the assignment so that I could take summer courses toward a degree in religious studies. He approved my request. I chose to enroll at the University of San Francisco (USF).

The program focused on the teachings of Vatican II. Lecturers with international reputations in scripture, theology, and science served as faculty. It was the perfect program for me. And yes, I had followed the journey charted by my kite dream back on the farm and found my way to San Francisco. My odyssey was taking me to the West Coast.

I was especially thrilled when I heard my younger sister, Mary Jo, who had joined the Sisters of the Visitation Order, and one of her friends could accompany me when I drove from Iowa to San Francisco for my classes. It was a great opportunity for me to get to know her better. She told me, "I never really knew you because you left home when I was a little girl." I was also pleased she was in the convent and we would have an opportunity to share our religious life experiences.

Mary Jo collected rock samples in the Sangre de Cristo mountains for a class she taught, loading them in the trunk of the car. After three days of travel touring the Taos Pueblo and driving through Death Valley we arrived at my other sister Margaret's apartment in Palo Alto. Margaret had moved to the West coast after she left the convent several years before. The four of us had a memorable reunion dinner that evening. I drove to San Francisco the next day to register for classes in my program.

The summer program at USF presented challenging, substantive courses. I gradually found I couldn't put new wine in old wine skins back at Wahlert. The teachers and students were excited about the new teachings and changes in the Church. On the other hand, the administrators and some of my fellow priests had been trained under the authority-oriented tradition of the church and were actively avoiding any change initiated by Vatican II.

I must admit I was sandpapered a lot by the "old guard," but I learned to listen and separate emotions from understanding. I was constantly answering the question, "Why must we change?" Or more seriously being accused of being a radical because I was expressing uncomfortable ideas. In response to one of the changes coming from the Vatican Council, the bishop of the diocese sent a directive to pastors to instruct their parishioners about the background and meaning of the " kiss of peace." It is a gesture, such as shaking hands with those near you at Mass and offering a wish, "May the peace of Christ be with you." The pastors were instructed to deliver these sermons over the course of the following three Sundays.

We had scheduled a Mass for the 550 members of the sophomore class when the letter was sent out. All the religious education instructors of the sophomores had already prepared the students in their classes the week before the scheduled Mass, carefully following the bishop's instructions for the exchange of peace. Students understood its symbolism. Many expressed thanks for friendship, hugged a close friend, and even apologized for past snub or unkind words. It was an inspiring moment to see teenagers come alive; often they sat passively during Mass. They expressed the real meaning of community at Mass.

Right after Mass I was called to the office the school's administrator, Father Raker, because I had not observed the timeline spelled out by the bishop: "All the pastors will be upset because you preempted the three weeks required by the bishop's orders," he scolded me. "I don't want any radicals on my faculty for them to complain about," Somehow, the bishop's orders, "three weeks," became more important than the purpose of the directive preparing people for the meaning of the kiss of peace. The new wine of meaningfulness did not fit well into the old wine skin of authority and rules.

I was in a real time of turmoil, finally moving away from just teaching rules and practices of the institution. Could I still wear the collar if I wasn't convinced that I should be loyal to the rules? I was deeply troubled and began questioning my current role.

The opportunity came the next summer when I returned to USF. My course on Teilhard de Chardin's writings had an enormous impact on me. Teilhard, a Jesuit priest and anthropologist, espoused an evolution in personal spiritual growth as well as the biological theory of evolution as we know it. His teachings brought me back to religion as living one's life following the gospel. His writings are a synthesis of science and theology. They were an inspiration for my ongoing search on how to integrate theology and science.

The in-depth class discussions carried over to many after class conversations and led to a special friendship with one of my classmates. Often when at lunch in the cafeteria, the name of Sister Eleanah from Boston came up in conversation. It finally dawned on me Eleanah was Sister Eleanor Dunfey who was taking the Teilhard course with me. We had chatted briefly after class the first couple of meetings. I felt there was something special about her, but I maintained my clerical demeanor. Then Eleanor approached me to chair a class discussion of her paper. Not only did I agree, but I also sensed the feeling was mutual. Still "guarding" my feelings, I asked her to iron a shirt I needed for a gathering the next evening. She agreed and I felt more comfortable meeting with her. I was now joining others talking about Eleanah in my conversations in the cafeteria.

As our presentations in class continued, our conversations took on a more personal tone. We had concerns about the same issues: Where the church was headed; the Encyclical, "Humanae Vitae"; the church becoming more aware of contemporary issues such as civil rights, poverty, and educating the laity; celibacy and married clergy.

On weekends I visited my sister Margaret in Palo Alto. I invited Eleanor and her roommate, Sister Nancy, to join me on one of those visits. We had a delightful dinner and evening. The next day Margaret called me and said, "Jim, I really like Eleanor. I liked her ideas about the Church. Please invite her again." That was my sister's nod of approval to Eleanor's and my friendship.

Now I was experiencing more than friendship. I took Eleanor and her roommate to the Cliff House for Irish Coffee as a special thank you toward the end of the summer. I didn't know at that time Eleanor's Irish family were restaurateurs and specialized in that drink. We laughed together and enjoyed our Irish Coffee as she told me their story. At one point Nancy excused herself: "I'm going to go over to watch the seals." Nancy was one member of a close circle of friends who recognized that we had a special bond.

The summer session ended shortly after. We walked to the Japanese Tea Garden in Golden Gate Park and planned how to continue our conversations during the months ahead. She was remaining on campus to finish her degree, and I was returning to Iowa in my faculty role. We decided to send tapes, write letters, and call one another.

Our bond deepened as our friendship grew. We discovered we were both dealing with the same dilemma—our commitment to the church, our current religious status, and future decisions. These conversations sealed our trust. We both talked extensively about the possibility of moving on from our roles as priest and nun and the next steps. I had to inform my bishop and decide whether I would request laicization from the Vatican.

Eleanor and I corresponded through the following year. The telephone conversation I remember most occurred over the Christmas break. Eleanor had returned to her home in New Hampshire.

On Christmas Day, in the late afternoon I called her. During our conversation, I was able to say hello to her mother for the first time. Her mother told me she looked forward to seeing me in New

Hampshire. I had a special smile on my face later when I joined in my own family Christmas celebration.

When I had returned to Wahlert after that summer session of 1969, I had immersed myself in my role and decided I would finalize the decision to stay or to leave. During the fall, I discovered Teens Encounter Christ (TEC), an initiation to the Christian experience I was seeking for the students and myself. TEC was a gathering of senior students led by a team of priests, nuns and lay adults. I attended a TEC and became convinced it was the program I was searching for. I brought it to our school. Students attending a TEC gathered for three days and focused on their lives, Christian values, celebration of Mass and the sacraments, and how they could lead their lives in a Christian manner.

TEC really helped students. One of my students, Ginny, made a TEC and it changed her life. She was one of my senior students searching for answers and came to my office often to discuss Sunday Mass attendance and other practices, such as no meat on Friday. After several meetings she decided it was time to make a TEC. When she returned from the weekend, she came to my office and wanted to get her peers more involved in living the Christian life. Reflecting on her own grandmother who was living alone and needed assistance, she started a group to visit the elderly who lived alone. I remember her sharing that she had 20 students visiting and assisting elderly persons. TEC had helped Ginny move beyond observing rules to finding a way to live the gospel message. As I observed Ginny and so many of the students discover the richness of the Christian message, I began to reflect on my role.

I remembered one Sunday after Mass, when my father had asked the priest if he could "break the Sabbath" to harvest oats. The weather forecast had been rain for four days, which would affect the quality of the crop. My father was given permission. I was bothered because my father had made a logical, practical decision, but he felt he needed the permission of the priest to do so. The priest had grown up on a farm and understood my father's request; another priest without that experience might not have said yes.

Dilemma

More and more, I began to question whether I could continue to live a role bound by these kinds of institutional norms and rules. Which is more important: observing the law to attend Mass every Sunday to be saved, or understanding attending Mass contributes to leading a life based on Christian principles that open the door to salvation? TEC had been positive, but I found it difficult to change ideas, values, and behaviors in the institution I was representing. While words matter, even the most carefully crafted creeds, laws and rules do not always carry over to one's acts and life. As did Ginny, I discovered Christianity is a heartfelt commitment.

Working with the students was an exciting and learning experience. My generation was oriented towards institutions and following the rules. The students were searching for meaning in their lives. They would ask, "Why do we have to go to Mass every Sunday? Why can't I just go and meditate in the woods and show respect for Him?" The rule of weekly attendance was so deeply engrained that it was difficult to explain the importance of community and the grace derived by attendance.

The head of the house called me aside one day at school. "I don't understand what is happening on these TECs. The kids come back so high." I suggested he join one of the weekends. His response was, "I am too old for that kind of emotional religious experience. I prefer the old-time retreats and quiet times to meditate." I was sad for him. It was so much easier for me, too, when I just followed the rules, practices, and printed prayers. But I'd lose so much if I did.

I was torn between my eight years of training, my loyalty to the teachings of the church and my TEC experiences. After talking with two students, totally excited about their TEC, I drove home in an emotional maelstrom. After dinner I went to my room and tried to read. I could not focus on the article, and my head was beating. I went out, got in the car and drove to a lookout place to see the farm where I had grown up. I felt emotionally drained realizing my world, beginning with the farm rituals and now my priesthood years, might be ending. I knew my father and mother had adapted to previous changes in my life. Now I was about to ask them to adapt to the most difficult change for all three of us: my leaving the priesthood.

I started the car and drove aimlessly. Then I searched for a telephone booth and called Eleanor. She answered, and her voice was heaven sent. I was able to tell her about my sense of loss. I was for the first time saying out loud that I knew in my heart I had made my decision. Listening with great empathy, she reassured me that we would fashion a new future together. I hung up the phone, relieved, realizing I had twice before changed my path in life, leaving behind the farm and a career in medicine. I now felt a new security about my decision..

As fall morphed into winter, my priest friend Vince Jestice, Superintendent of the Diocesan Catholic Schools, called and asked if I would like to go to a movie. That night during the movie he shared that he was leaving the priesthood. He expressed his doubts about the authenticity of the Bible and other teachings of the Church. I was shocked. I had always looked upon Vince as an intellectual stalwart and turned to him often with questions of my own. I shared my concerns about the role of the priest. He listened quietly but had no advice. We said good night, and I left confused about Vince but more deeply grounded in my own decision.

Following the Christmas break, I continued to have lingering doubts about the decision to leave the priesthood. In some ways it was like the decision in my senior year in college. The Catholic culture of my farm and family life had led me to the priesthood. The seminary was a safe and respected continuation of my early life. Where would my new experience lead after the priesthood? I was grappling with the question, "Could I lead a better Christian life outside the role of priest?"

The decision came in May 1970. I shared with my parents that I had decided to leave the priesthood. They, of course, were shocked and saddened. Vince and another of my classmates had announced their decisions earlier, so at least my parents were now aware of priests leaving.

Even though my parents were stunned at first, their response was magnanimous. I remember my father asking, "Is there anything we can do? Is it the current assignment?" Despite their disappointment, they were very affirming. "You have to do what is best for your life." I felt compassion for my parents, my mother losing her son as a priest and my father now having to deal with another change of direction in my life. He had accepted my not being a farmer; now I was asking him to accept this decision. I was grateful they didn't object.

In May I met with my bishop to inform him I was requesting a leave of absence from the priesthood. Unbelievably, he informed me that he had heard rumors that I was dating one of the nuns on the faculty at Wahlert. He asked that I write a formal letter to the bishop promising not to communicate with that person by letter or any other form during the next year. I readily agreed and later wrote the letter responding to his request. The rumor was just that, a rumor. The person the bishop had heard about was, in fact, a colleague and good friend at Wahlert. The bishop asked no questions. He had his "plan" for me set ahead of the meeting. Had he asked, I would have shared the real story of "Eleanah," the woman I would later marry. As I left his office, I met a close friend who worked in the Chancery. He asked how the interview had gone. I told him of the request for the letter based on the rumors. He replied, "Good. Write the letter. It's sad he believes rumors." The remaining time in Dubuque was as difficult for my parents as challenging for me. Everyone we met would invariably ask about my leaving

As a boy in Iowa flying my kite, I had always dreamed of living in New England. After much discussion in our correspondence, Eleanor and I decided we were both leaving and came up with a plan. I would go to New England to work out the final steps of my decision. With her help, I requested residency in a parish in Manchester, New Hampshire. From there she and I would seek employment and define our future. Although we had developed a deep personal relationship, each of us still needed to work through many personal outcomes of our decisions, emotional and otherwise. Would we get married? At that point we really did not know each other all that well. We'd have to find that out in the year ahead living near each other.

After school closed in early June, I packed my belongings into the trunk of my one possession, a Plymouth Fury. My parents agreed to store books and some other items until I resettled. I shared my decision with the other priests on the faculty. While they were accepting, only one really was truly supportive, Bill "Ben" Franklin. During the months leading up to my decision, he was my mentor and helped me work through the decision to leave. We would remain close friends after I moved to New England and long beyond.

Before leaving Vianney House, Father Clarence Raker, the head of the house, invited me to have one last martini with him. The conversation was very pedestrian, but he did ask why I was leaving. I replied, "One martini and a last-minute conversation are not adequate to explain my decision." We parted friends, and I said I would keep in touch.

Leaving Vianney House, I took one last wistful look back at my home of the past seven years. In this moment of mixed feelings, I tried to remember the happy times, started the car and headed for a quick visit with my parents to let them know I would stop by the next day before I left for New Hampshire. I didn't look back. My room was empty. I was moving on.

Chapter 37

Taking Leave of Dubuque

On that June 20, 1970, I was still working through the feelings of being rooted, having prestige among my peers for my accomplishments, and having a meaningful role in the community. I collected my thoughts. Yes, I could begin again. I was a teacher and had a degree in biology. That would serve me well in getting a job. But what would it be like to transition from 12 years of celibate living to an intimate relationship? Could I adapt to new geographic, cultural and personal experiences? I told myself, "Yes, I can."

We planned that Eleanor would fly from San Francisco into the Twin Cities after her graduation. After picking her up we would drive to Dubuque. Eleanor and I agreed to meet my parents before we left for the East Coast. We wanted this chance for them to share their feelings about our decisions and plans before leaving Dubuque. My hope was that they would continue to understand and be supportive. They had shared my change from med school to the seminary. Now they had to deal with losing a vital part of their lives, my role as a priest in the church. The priest's role was the link to God and salvation for them.

Before I knew it, I was at the airport meeting Eleanor. As she walked towards me after leaving the plane, I felt I had found a new sense of purpose in my life. Her smile transported me back to those earlier days in San Francisco looking forward to meeting after class. As we hugged, I experienced a release from my previous months of agonizing. Now my decision was real and together we would share it with my parents.

After a quick update on the flight and collecting her bags, we set off to drive to my parents' home. In the excitement of finally meeting after months of phone calls and letters, our conversation was an uninterrupted flow of catching up, of talking about our leave takings, and of addressing how we were going to handle the conversation with my parents.

There were other dimensions to my parents' concerns I had to share in person with Eleanor before this meeting. My relationship with my father had been strained from my early years until I entered the seminary. He was a very religious man and highly respected the priesthood. When I made the decision to enter the seminary, he saw the priesthood as a higher calling than following in his footsteps. Now he had to deal with another of my decisions, our relationship. My father never saw life on the farm as confining; he was able to move beyond traditional patterns and introduce new farming practices. When I mentioned I was thinking of leaving the priesthood, he intuitively knew how I felt, that I did feel constrained by what I was doing, and I needed to make a change.

I also made Eleanor aware of some of my mother's concerns. Being the mother of a priest was every Catholic mother's prayer. And now I was leaving. It would call for a great deal of courage and acceptance of my decision, as many in our small farming community would question it.

Mom had also experienced two of her daughters joining the convent and leaving. When Margaret had suffered convulsions from the mercury poisoning as a little girl, Mom had not only prayed for recovery, but promised she would encourage Margaret to serve God in a special way if she recovered. After she graduated from high school, Margaret had joined the convent and later left. Mom shared with me that she struggled at first, but then accepted that Margaret had now chosen to serve as a teacher in a way she had never imagined. Seven years later Mary Jo, my second sister, also left. Mom now spoke proudly of MaryJo studying for her PhD and preparing for her upcoming marriage. My mother recognized in her daughters how she had developed her own potential as a nurse.

We arrived at my parents' home. After a warm welcome, we were taken aback as Dad immediately told of their previous evening's experience. A priest they knew, along with his housekeeper, had gone for a ride and engaged in more than viewing the scenery. Embarrassed, and their clothing in disarray, they arrived unexpectedly at my parents' door. They trusted my parents to discreetly handle their indiscretion. My parents communicated to us, without any further commentary, what had happened before they arrived at the house.

Dad summarized the situation in this manner, "I don't want you to stay in the priesthood and live like that. I would much prefer that you leave and marry."

As they listened to our plans, it was clear that they were open and supportive of our relationship. Their only caution was "Don't rush into marriage." We assured them that our real concern was to take our time transitioning, to get jobs, and most importantly, to deepen our relationship. We promised them only then would we consider marriage. They gave us a wholehearted send off and we ventured East on our new journey. When we stopped the next day in Cleveland for lunch, I reminisced, "Would you believe, I am about to realize the third of my kite flying dreams? I'm going to live in New England." After shopping for some non-clerical clothing, I had Eleanor help me choose the colors of my shirt and pants or I would have chosen black. Then we drove on to the Yankee Drummer Inn in Auburn, Massachusetts.

I had only spoken with Eleanor's mother on the phone. Now, as soon as I had parked the car, Eleanor and I bolted out and rushed up a slight hill on the lawn where we were greeted with warm hugs by Eleanor's mother, her brother Roy, and his wife Ruth. The next hours flew by as we recapped the visit with my parents and our trip East, including our shopping excursion.

That evening we gathered for our welcome dinner. Eleanor's mother toasted to acceptance and warm conversation with a *"Cead mile Failte"*, a hundred thousand welcomes. Nanna, as I now came to know her, capped off the evening saying, "I now have a ninth son Jim" as we all shared Irish Coffee, a Dunfey specialty. Although Eleanor told me I would be welcomed warmly, I had been nervous about this first meeting. Any anxiety I might have experienced was totally dispelled.

Eleanor had asked her mother for some quiet time after we arrived to talk and share our plans, so the next day we retreated to Hampton to hide away at Lamie's Inn to Mrs. Dunfey's cozy apartment. On the trip to Hampton we joined in singing a medley of favorites of her family's songs. I joined with them as I knew several of the lyrics. This songfest took me back to my college and camp counselor days, and I was already feeling at home.

The hideaway turned out to be more of a long series of introductions to Eleanor's 11 siblings, their spouses, and her nieces and nephews over the next two weeks. They came to welcome Eleanor home and to check out her Midwestern escort. Everybody surmised she was leaving the convent although she had not announced it. They were very supportive and invited Eleanor and me for many visits. It seemed like old home week in Dubuque with my family.

Although I had a vast Iowa lineage, the Dunfey family members were a countless never-ending series of faces and names. On one occasion, Eleanor and I attended an opening of one of the family's hotels. As the valet took my keys, a man approached me and said, "You must be Jim. I am Paul, Eleanor's brother. Walter (another brother) gave me the 30-second fill in on you." Taken aback, I answered, "I thought I was worth at least 60 seconds."

Job Seeking

During those weeks we weren't just socializing. We were anxious about getting jobs. Fortunately, I found a biology teaching job opening in Vermont. We set off in late June for Burlington, where I had a good interview with the department head at Burlington High School and he introduced me to the principal. After they had a momentary meeting, we went back to his office. He offered me the job and made a phone call to the State Department of Education to set up an appointment for my certification. I was elated and couldn't wait to share the news with Eleanor. That night at dinner, we toasted my new role as a biology teacher and planned our trip to Montpelier the next day.

When we arrived at the State Office in Montpelier to complete my paperwork, the registrar met with Eleanor and informed her about an opening for an English teacher at South Burlington High School. Eleanor expressed her interest and the registrar called the department head to set up an interview. Eleanor met with her and the principal the next morning. They offered her the position.

In two days, we had changed roles from priest and nun to public school teachers. Before one month elapsed, we had gotten jobs, rented and furnished apartments, and received approval from both of our families.

One last visit with Eleanor's brother Paul's family at their lake home culminated my summer experience with the Dunfey family. Gail, Eleanor's niece, welcomed me with a family game. She "hypnotized me" asking silly questions about my life. To my chagrin, her whole family broke into laughter as they listened to my answers. At the same time as she rubbed my cheeks, chin and forehead checking if I was hypnotized, she colored my face creating a clown appearance. Gail later characterized my stay during the summer as, "creating a personal relationship with each of the Dunfey family members."

In August Eleanor and I moved to Vermont for our new adventure, Eleanor to Burlington and I to Colchester. The sun rose over Mount Mansfield in the East each morning and set in the West over the Adirondacks. Those sunrises and sunsets were the inspirations for a new chapter in my life, together with Eleanor.

Eleanor and Me in Vermont
Winter 1970

CHAPTER 38

Moonlight in Vermont

It is 2018 and I am in our Exeter, NH apartment. I raise my hand to quell a morning yawn. I roll back the covers and sit on the edge of the bed, squinting through my half-closed eyes. I watch dreamily as the Exeter River water courses its way into the tidal basin of the Swampscott. The soothing sound of the river swishes me back to a fall evening in 1970, our first year in Vermont. I hear Frank Sinatra softly crooning, "People who meet in this romantic setting are hypnotized by the lovely evening..." I knew I had charted the right course with Eleanor as I listened to Sinatra singing softly as a backdrop.

At that earlier time in Burlington, I drove across town to join Eleanor for dinner. She had told me earlier she had a surprise meal; I suspected Chicken Florentine, my favorite.

I recalled my days on the faculty at Wahlert High School when Mom would call and invite me for dinner. I relished those nights. I remembered hearing what was happening with the Battons and all the neighbors. I never knew how Mom did it, but she was up to-date on every family happening of my brothers' families although she never seemed to talk with us. Those dinners were more informative than the local newspaper, *The Telegraph Herald*.

My nephew, Paul, characterized her uncanny ability to gather news. He comments:

"Remember how Gerene Freiburger used to know everything about everyone's' lives over multiple counties around Dubuque? "Fannie's cousin's neighbor's daughter on the farm with the big oak tree northwest of Zwingle got engaged to Emit's nephew's brother's barber from down on 3rd street in Maquoketa..." Now, just imagine if she had lived in an era with social media? Imagine her with access to the constant stream of information about everyone's lives that we currently have? She would have been totally addicted, or exploded with how much information she would have had to share with everyone... I'm still trying to wrap my mind around that mind-blowing concept.

According to my dad, the party line telephone they had on the farm was essentially the same thing as social media, so maybe it wouldn't have been that different!"

Reminiscent of, but not nearly as far reaching, my conversations with Mom at home, my dinners with Eleanor were an update on our new daily happenings, friends and family.

After finishing the main course, we agreed we both liked our classwork and loved Burlington. Then lightheartedly, Eleanor described how her mother at 79 years of age had mischievously submitted her application responding to a chauffeur ad for Dunfey (her family's) hotels. Eleanor said, "I am not surprised. My mother always welcomed and thrived in every new stage of her life. I'll bet the hotel management had a laugh about it."

I helped Eleanor clear the dishes. Returning to the table as she prepared dessert, I thought of her mother's lightheartedness in applying for a chauffeur's job. I lost my train of thought when I saw the apple pie ala mode Eleanor had set before me.

Giving my post-pie stomach a pat of satisfaction, I cleared the dishes and talked about the next day. Then I explained I had a stack of papers to read. I thanked Eleanor, kissed her good night and left.

On the drive home, I thought back to Eleanor's mother's job application. It reminded me that she and my parents had openly accepted and developed new stages in their lives. I reminisced about the last conversation with my parents as we were leaving Dubuque. They had asked, "What are your plans?" They had wondered aloud if I had found a direction for my life after passing up a career in medicine and leaving the priesthood.

For the first time since coming East in June, I realized their far-sightedness led me to reflect on their question. They had taken a farm that was foreclosed on by a bank and charted a whole new life. Without realizing it, I was following their example. I was leaving a past behind and charting my future. Mom and Dad had made a life together; could Eleanor and I do the same?

Thinking back, I wondered if all my experiences, events and decisions prepared me for the future?

"Is teaching biology preparing me for the future?"

I turned on the radio, the evening news was ending. There was a brief interlude of silence and the soothing voice of Frank Sinatra sounded, "Pennies in the stream... Moonlight in Vermont." I tapped my fingers on the steering wheel as he sang on. "People who meet in this romantic setting are so hypnotized by the lovely evening summer breeze..." I was choked up! When I reached my apartment, I immediately called Eleanor and told her about "Moonlight in Vermont" and my thoughts about teaching biology. "I'm wondering," I quipped, "Do you think there might be a chauffeur's job in my future?"

The next morning when I arrived at school, two teachers were huddled in the faculty room, discussing the teacher contract.

"Tell me about the contract. Are there problems?" I had never dealt with negotiated contracts. As a priest I had been assigned by the bishop. My salary, housing, and benefits were always provided.

They stated that the teachers had last negotiated two years earlier and they saw no indication the school committee would review the salary and benefits. They did not want to continue in this frozen state of employment. I thanked them for sharing and walked away, upset that I was so naïve about the politics underlying contract negotiations. I hadn't felt this embarrassed since the episode of my blue shirt as a freshman in high school. If I wanted to continue to teach, I better do some homework.

It was also time for me to deal with a far more complicated agreement. I applied to Rome for a dispensation from the priesthood. I was ready to do that. However, after mailing the letter, I agonized whether over next few months the Vatican would accept my request.

The official letter arrived from the Vatican January 1971, signed by His Holiness Pope Paul VI. What a feeling of relief after months of rules, procedures and finalizing my decision!

Earlier in the summer Eleanor had signed the necessary documents releasing her from her vows. She, too, felt relieved to have finalized her decision. Now we had moved beyond making decisions about our pasts and could go forward together with our lives. We had both taken our commitments to priesthood and religious life very seriously. I had experienced success in my eight years in the priesthood and Eleanor never regretted her 12 years as a nun. We both wanted to remain in good standing as lay members of the church and now, almost a year and a half later, we had reached a whole new understanding of the direction of our lives. One of our favorite reflections described this moment best: "For all that has been, thanks. For all that will be, yes." (Dag Hammarskjold, second secretary general of the UN).

I felt a new surge of freedom and decided I would ask Eleanor to marry me. She had shared once that she did not want an engagement ring. As a celibate I had never been faced with such a personal choice of gifts. Serendipitously, a good friend came to my rescue. Hugh Gallen, the future governor of New Hampshire, had asked Eleanor and me to act as surrogate parents to his daughter Kathy, a freshman at the University of Vermont. She came for dinner on several occasions, and I felt comfortable asking her to help me with the shopping. We selected a charm bracelet with a diamond. The stage was set; now I had to figure out the right time and place.

I was so preoccupied with the engagement moment that I forgot to look at the calendar. Eleanor called to tell me she was planning a candlelight dinner to celebrate Valentine's Day and the arrival of my dispensation. Without planning, the opportunity to propose had presented itself!

During dinner, the moment arrived. Eleanor asked, "Is it even possible both of our 'papers' have actually arrived? Can you believe it?" Startled by the question, I was overwhelmed by my feelings and humbly answered, "I have been thinking of the two of us!"

It was an exhilarating moment; a totally emotional release after the months of waiting. We both sat teary eyed for a moment. After all my planning, I was speechless. I stood up, went over, and gave her the gift-wrapped bracelet. She cautiously opened the box, lifted out the bracelet, slowly viewed the charm diamond, and I helped her put on her wrist. We hugged, kissed, and her eyes said "yes." This moment of silent acceptance eclipsed all the struggles with the decisions that had led us to this moment.

I called my parents to tell them I had asked Eleanor to marry me. My mother said, "We want to come out and be there to celebrate with you. Let us know when you have set a date for the wedding." I assured her it would be a time when they could be away from the farm for a few days.

I thought back to special times in my early years. I remembered sharing my college thesis with my father and his warmly accepting my writing about his work and the farm. He had been proud when I became a priest and stood with me when I left the priesthood. He accepted the promise not to rush into marriage that Eleanor and I made as we said goodbye when leaving Dubuque. Now my parents' willingness to share in the celebration of our future sent shivers up my spine. They both recognized that I valued my roots and all that they meant to me.

The following weekend we visited Eleanor's mother. With a knowing smile when Eleanor told her the news, she said, "Let's celebrate this wonderful news with a special dinner tonight." She toasted to our happiness; then we discussed the date we had chosen, a date that would work for each family's schedule, as well as our school term. We would get married on August 7, 1971.

There was one more challenging step before our marriage, meeting with the chancellor of the Manchester diocese to sign my dispensation papers and go forward with our wedding. The meeting began with a cordial discussion while I signed the documents Then he spelled out the bishop's rules for weddings of former priests. He informed me the bishop preferred that we keep the upcoming wedding private, limited to the groom, bride, and two witnesses.

Wow! Once again rules were preempting a Sacrament's true meaning. I had just signed a document dispensing me from the priesthood, and now the bishop was imposing rules as if I were still required to obey him. Moreover, these directives were contrary to the public nature of marriage. In my gut I wondered if I could ever leave the past behind and envision a whole new future.

At this point I asked Eleanor to come join us. Hearing his conditions, she asked, "Doesn't the church require a couple, before marriage, to publicly proclaim their intent to marry for three Sundays in the parishes where they reside? My family in New Hampshire is extensive, and probably one of the more public families in New England. How can the Bishop require that a sacrament, publicly proclaiming the union of two people, be conducted behind closed doors?"

The chancellor was taken aback by Eleanor's statement. She had directly addressed the Bishop's rules and clearly stated the church's teaching and practice of the Sacrament of Marriage. It was the first of many times in our life together that she played an important role in our decision making.

Eleanor suggested we move the ceremony to Burlington, Vermont. Apparently never thinking of that option, the Chancellor showed relief and immediately picked up the phone and called the Burlington Bishop's office. That bishop approved, and we moved the wedding to Vermont.

My first thought was how times had changed. I went back to the role the pastor of our youth, Father Long, had played in our family. He had supported my mother and her efforts to educate us kids, breaking the traditional mold of our just following my father's and his father's farming career. Now Eleanor and I were issuing a challenge to the chancellor of the diocese to move the church forward, look beyond rules, and honoring the real meaning of our marriage.

We spent the spring looking for a house. We settled on a comfortable ranch house on Lakewood Drive in Shelburne, which became the wedding house. Eleanor, and her mother, sisters, along with her oldest brother Roy prepared for the ceremony there.

My sister Margaret and her husband John arrived from England and their travel plans prevented them from staying for the wedding. I was pleased when they volunteered to help us move our belongings from the two apartments and paint the interior of our new home.

My parents, my brother Tom and I walked down the aisle on August 7, 1971. I was again sharing one of the most emotional moments of my life with them. How did this even happen?

Eleanor and I exchanged vows in the intimate setting of the Cathedral Chapel. Her family, my family, and our friends joined in singing *"Today," "There's a New World Somewhere,"* and *"We've Only Just Begun."* Our families joined our celebration welcoming and supporting us as we faced our future life together.

The Wedding
Kay Dunfey (Bridesmaid), Roy Dunfey, Eleanor, Monsignor Kenney
(Celebrant), Me, Father Wm. Franklin (Co-Celebrant),
and Tom (Best Man)

Roy Dunfey (Eleanor's Brother), Eleanor's Mother, Eleanor,
Me, Mom, Dad

Sharing our wedding celebration

The romantic setting of our Vermont wedding reached afar. We flew to Switzerland for our honeymoon. Waiting at the baggage area in the Zurich airport, we were mystified when Eleanor's luggage didn't arrive—It was sitting neatly packed in our living room at home. Later looking at our Switzerland pictures, we were able to distinguish each day of our honeymoon by one of the two sets of clothing Eleanor had purchased to replace her missing wardrobe.

CHAPTER 39

Home Again

Following our honeymoon, Eleanor and I both began our second year of teaching in South Burlington and Burlington High School, respectively. Reaching back to my dreams growing up on the farm, I began to feel the same yearning to explore whether a new "field" lay ahead for me.

That unsettled feeling became more pronounced as I heard a growing concern among the teachers discussing the upcoming contract negotiation. The faculty had met, selected representatives, and sent a notice to the school committee to set a date to negotiate.

At the October negotiation meeting, four faculty members presented our requests. When they finished, the negotiator for the school committee did not speak. He reached under his seat, pulled out a paper bag, and handed the four presenters lollipops (suckers). He stood up and left, adjourning the meeting without responding to the presentation. I, along with the other teachers attending, sat in stunned silence, waiting for someone from the school committee to respond. They also exited the room. We teachers remained seated, feeling totally humiliated.

Suddenly, I was jolted back to my past. Those in charge had been overly zealous in imposing rules and policies. Now I felt a similar knot tightening in my stomach. I'd hoped a teaching job would set me on a path going forward.

I left the meeting depressed and uncertain about continuing as a teacher. After several conversations with Eleanor, I realized that although I was having a good experience in the classroom, a larger issue loomed. In my previous life as a priest, I had experienced respect. I had exercised leadership in developing curriculum and made classrooms more satisfying for teachers. The negotiation meeting reminded me that I had not only lost the past but now I could not see an opportunity for a leadership role in the future.

Searching for a direction in the spring of 1972, I enrolled in graduate courses at the University of Vermont. Four weeks into my studies, the Dean of the Graduate Educational Administration Department called me into his office. "I have nominated you for a graduate fellowship, an internship working with innovative projects funded by Title III federal grants in the State Department of Education." When I shared the news with Eleanor, we agreed the timing and opportunity were perfect. The next day I announced I would be resigning in June. A door opened for my future I enrolled as a full-time graduate student in the summer session.

In September the position began in Montpelier, a three-day-a-week commute. began. During that year I traversed Vermont from Newport to Bennington, supervising 30 exciting, creative student-oriented projects funded and under my supervision. I recalled my years at Wahlert High School and realized helping young people find their way gave me the greatest feeling of satisfaction.

In this program my favorite project involved a devoted teacher, Lynette Denny, who led fifth grade students in writing poems. I sat intrigued, watching as Lynette played her guitar and sang their poetry lyrics transposed to music. The program was so successful that I extended her visiting role to several other schools. Lynette suffered from macular degeneration in both eyes and traveled with a service dog. She summarized the project, stating, "I loved doing the poetry and music, but the most meaningful part of my working with the children was sharing their interest and enthusiasm about a service dog being my eyes."

CHAPTER 40

Starting a Family of Our Own

Our family odyssey began with Joel's birth in Vermont. Filled with expectation, we spent the summer and fall preparing for his arrival. Eleanor and her mother enjoyed happy days shopping for baby furniture and a stroller. I spent my time painting and preparing the nursery in our small ranch house.

My parents were ecstatic with the news, especially when I shared that Father "Ben" Franklin, our dear family friend from my Wahlert High School days, had agreed to come out for the baptism just as he had for our wedding.

I stood beside Eleanor in the delivery room, a surgical mask not concealing the tears in my eyes as our first born made his entry into the world. I turned to witness the joy on Eleanor's face, noted the studied gazes on the 25 faces of the student nurses standing as observers, and heard the doctor proclaim, "This is a long one, 21 inches. A boy!"

I purchased a Super 8 camera and asked a friend to video Joel's Baptism. Students in our CCD class and several family members attended. Our fledgling photographer friend took the request literally, filming every minute for the next hour and a half, including the trip to and from our house. We had to run the 8mm film for a while to find the actual baptism, a 30-second clip.

CHAPTER 41

My Journey Continues

In the spring of 1973, the dean again called me into his office. He explained, "The University of Vermont is initiating a cooperative partnership with the University of Connecticut doctoral program in Educational Administration. We wondered if you would be interested in being our first candidate." I sat in stunned silence as he continued: "When I inform them, their staff will schedule a follow-up interview. We feel confident you meet all the requirements for this program. It includes a fellowship providing financial support."

For the next couple of days Eleanor and I discussed the pros and cons, agreeing I should pursue the opportunity. The importance of this decision prompted me to meet with Fred Jervis, a professional consultant who had counseled Eleanor's family on business and family matters. After a brief discussion he asked, "Ten years from now, what do you envision yourself doing that will allow you to achieve the same kind of respect and leadership you earned in the past?" Although blind, Fred's keen insights helped me in forming yet another vision for my life. The move to Connecticut made sense as an important first step in creating that future. I made an appointment with the dean to accept the offer. Fred Jervis had helped me turn an unexpected opportunity into the cornerstone for reshaping my professional future.

I enrolled in the doctoral program at the University of Connecticut in September 1973, the farm and the priesthood in my rear-view mirror. When I called my parents to tell them about my new venture, Mom, who early on was an advocate for my education, said "I always knew you would be a doctor."

I chose community education as my major. My courses would emphasize "a dynamic process by which individuals within a community identify local resources and coordinate them through the public schools and government services to meet community needs and problems." I had to choose courses to fulfill the program requirements. I enjoyed making appointments with education, sociology, and research professors to develop a course of study. The research instructor said, "Community education sounds very innovative but a stretch for a quantitative research project. Come back and see me when you are ready to discuss your dissertation topic." I left him realizing I had some challenging work ahead.

Sitting in one of my first classes, I drifted back to Asbury and the role my father had played in our community. I began my program envisioning what skills I could use to work with leaders like him to plan and develop schools as the centerpiece of the community.

While the courses went well, my research project became a struggle. After many hours in the library, the research instructor accepted my topic. Sadly, later that month, he had a heart attack and died. I felt the loss of his support. I was fortunate, however. The dean respected him, became my advisor, and enthusiastically endorsed my research project. I began crafting the early chapters of my dissertation.

My study focused on the role of a citizen's advisory council in influencing a school committee in making its decisions. Choosing the City of Brockton, Massachusetts, I spent many days conducting surveys and collecting data. As I handed the data to my computer assistant for analysis, I felt a knot in my stomach.

"I hope you can make all those digital symbols yield a result justifying all my hours researching the topic and gathering data. "

In June of 1975, I defended my dissertation. As each advisor shook my hand and said, "Congratulations Dr. Freiburger," my head was still so immersed in the work of the past months that I really did not grasp my achievement. That moment came when I walked into our apartment and the dining area was strung with congratulatory streamers.

I gave Eleanor a hug and kiss, my thank you for her unending support. With a Rob Roy in hand, I touched Eleanor's glass of wine and toasted, "Thank you for making this possible. Here's to many more of these occasions in the future." Teary eyed, I heaved a deep sigh of relief and satisfaction.

Two years of work would now have a niche in a scholarly section of the university library. My parents came for my graduation. But more importantly, this chapter of my life concluded with the birth of our daughter Maria.

Graduation Day – June, 1976
Me, Joel, Maria, Eleanor

My Parenting Role Expands

Two and a half years after Joel's birth, we added another chapter in our family story in Connecticut. On a foggy morning on May 3, 1975, I stood again in the hospital's delivery room holding Eleanor's hand, welcoming a baby into our lives, Maria Catherine. Eleanor, also, ecstatic with her baby girl, cradled our newly blanketed 7 lb.16 oz bundle in her arms. Two days later, when Eleanor and baby arrived home from the hospital, Joel rode his toy dinosaur bike, peddling so fast he almost tipped over across the play area in our yard to greet them. He gave a big hug to his mother and cast a look of wonderment towards his blanketed little sister.

Eleanor wrote a special poem for Daddy:
In the foggy dawn
I clung to you for life.
The life you gave
Surged through me
And burst forth:
New life,
Sun filled morn – Maria!

With the arrival of Maria, we were now a family of four. Eleanor had survived the labor; I, the tedious toil of a dissertation; while Joel took on a new role as big brother. As a family we moved forward to the next stage in our adventure together.

Our Family Grows Up

By the age of seven, Joel was a foot taller than his classmates. Assessing a potential basketball career in his future, I introduced him to the game on a nearby court. After some dribbling practice, I decided shooting layups would make my coaching session more interesting. After demonstrating a layup, I walked Joel through the drive to the basket and layup. Tossing the ball to him, I directed him to dribble and shoot the layup. He did and at the end ran directly into the pole behind the basket. I had not shown him how to complete the drive and run past the pole.

I went over and knelt next to him. Stunned and in tears, he slowly sat up. The only visible damage was a bump on the forehead. I put my arms around him and helped him stand. We walked slowly home. On the way he asked, "Do I have to practice basketball again?" Chagrined, I answered , it would be his decision from now on. After that attempt, my coaching career with Joel came to an end. I was religated, thankfully, to the role of fan.

On the sidelines, I cheered his soccer and Little League baseball teams. Later he returned to basketball. Now when playing pickup with him on the court, my 6'7" son could stuff the ball back on me when I attempted a shot. I happily spent many nights sitting in the bleachers as a fan. I excelled at that.

Whether in a game or on his grandparents' farm in the early days,

Joel would have a mishap or two. On one visit while helping with the tractor, his grandfather asked him to push a clutch lever while attaching an implement. The attachment jumped quickly and caught Dad's finger, causing it to bleed. Joel saw the bleeding and thought the wound was serious. Although his finger was cut, Dad managed to hitch the implement, and then drove the tractor home. Joel slowly followed. He was deeply concerned and said to me, "I think I really hurt Grampa." A few minutes later Dad appeared, and Mom cleaned and bandaged the finger. Sensing Joel's concern, he came over to Joel, held out his hand and pointed, saying, "Now I have another special grandson's scar. Here is Eric's, here is Paul's, and now I have yours." Joel experienced the caring touch of his grandfather. The relief he felt didn't require a hug.

Many years later when Joel enrolled at the University of Notre Dame, we had many long drives and conversations, together. No longer were the exchanges abut mishaps, cut and bruises.

These were conversations about the not-so-obvious challenges. The most memorable occurred in a traffic jam at Scranton-Wilkes Barre Pennsylvania. Sitting surrounded by hundreds of cars, we had a chance to share some past experiences. Unmindful of the inch by inch movement of the car, Joel talked about our relationship and how I, and his mother, had served as role models. He connected his future plans to the values he had learned from me. That traffic jam gave us time, and I wasn't in a rush to get through it. Joel and I had a special bonding for the years ahead.

Maria

From her earliest years Maria kept us alert. She began walking at eight months. When she was 15 months old, I put her into her baby bed, lifted the side arm, said good night and went downstairs. Five minutes later, settled in a chair reading, I heard footsteps, looked up, and Maria called, "Hi Daddy." She had crawled over the side of the crib and was perched at the top of the flight of stairs.

By 1983, girls' soccer was gaining traction. Having never played the game, I went to parents' soccer training school, got introduced to the sport and then became her team's coach. I spent a lot of time learning new skills before practices and games. I would like to believe my four years as her coach helped lead her to become a star on her high school team.

One of my proudest moments as Maria's father, was her induction ceremony into the ACE/AmeriCorps program at the University of Notre Dame. She spent the following two years teaching in Jackson, MS, and also earned her Master's degree.

The summer of 2000 was the Freiburger wedding season. In July, I walked Maria down the aisle of Immaculate Conception Church in Portsmouth, NH, where she married Max Eisl. In September, we all shared in the joy of our son, Joel's marriage to Lanny Le in Chicago's Holy Name Cathedral. Being a close part of each of their family's lives has been the greatest gift of our lives.

A New Iowa Connection

I was standing in the bleachers cheering Joel's hit on his Little League baseball team. Another player's father next to me turned and said, "That was a great hit. By the way, my name is Bill McGeehan. I understand that you grew up in Dubuque." Bill, an executive in one of the Manchester banks, had just taken a new job as President of the American Trust and Savings Bank in Dubuque. This conversation in the bleachers initiated a string of events that extended from Manchester, NH, to my parents in Asbury, Iowa.

I met later with Bill and he told me that, growing up in New England, he had not learned much about the Midwest and farming. Could I recommend someone to inform him? Immediately I remembered tagging along when Dad had conducted tours of the farm, explaining soil conservation and his farming methods. I thought, why not my father? I suggested when Bill arrive in Dubuque that he meet Dad, a knowledgeable source about farming and its economics.

He followed up at the farm with my father and they spent a lot of time together. One day after walking the fields, Bill asked Dad why some stalks of corn had two ears, while most had only one. Dad's answer, "Those with two ears paid their rent." That became Bill's oft-repeated story.

The McGeehan connection gave rise to another Manchester-Dubuque bond. Sister Jeanette taught my daughter Maria in the second grade at St. Catherine's School. The two McGeehan children were a little older than Maria and had been Sr. Jeanette's students just a couple of years earlier. During that time, the brother and sister were in a serious car accident, so the dedicated Sr. Jeanette went to their home and taught them while they were housebound. She became one of the family. When the McGeehans moved to Dubuque, they invited Sister Jeanette to visit during the summer. Mrs. McGeehan had become a regular visitor to my parents' farm, where she bought eggs. Sister Jeanette accompanied her on one of those visits. When Dad heard she was Maria's teacher, he gave her a tractor ride and tour of the farm.

After Mass at St. Catherine Parish one Sunday in Manchester following her Iowa visit, Sister Jeanette came over and said, "I had a tractor ride with your father a couple of weeks ago." For the next several years, I would get an update on my parents and the farm from Sister Jeanette when she either visited the farm or saw my parents at Mass. Joel's baseball game and Maria's second grade teacher had created a whole new connection with my parents and Iowa roots.

Our Family
Max, Simon, Lanny, Emily, Eleanor, Jackson, Sophia,
Joel, Me, Willem, Maria
2019

CHAPTER 42

Losing My Father

Visiting my parent's farm every August was a tradition in our family. It was important to Eleanor and me that Joel and Maria spend time on the farm with Grandpa and Gramma and stay connected with my Iowa family. In April 1985, we decided to surprise Grandpa and Gramma Freiburger by going for a spring visit. But we were not prepared for the surprises we would have when we arrived there.

When traveling to Iowa, we usually flew into O'Hare and then caught a taxi to Elgin, and caught the train to Dubuque. This trip when we boarded the train, we had our first surprise. The conductor informed us the train service between Dubuque and Elgin was being discontinued at the end of April. That was not the kind of surprise that we wanted to hear. We all loved that train ride and have pictures of the conductor with Joel and Maria

A more appealing surprise arrived on Easter Sunday morning. My parents had picked us up at the train station the day before and we had great fun enjoying a warm spring day on the farm. When we woke up on Easter Sunday morning, not only had Easter baskets appeared, but the ground was covered with snow, our second surprise. I had never experienced snow at Easter on the farm.

During the week, Maria slept over at her cousin Lisa's house, and they returned in the morning to play at the farm. Gramma taught the girls how to gather eggs under a clucking chicken. Joel, who stayed overnight at his cousin Mark's home, also returned to the farm and they had some fun times together drawing figures on the tin machine shed roof.

The next day Joel helped Grampa riding on the tractor when he plowed in the field. Watching Joel and Grampa working together, I relived my plowing contest days with him. He was my hero and I always wanted to be like him. We had our rocky times, but I saw him in a new light through my own son's admiring eyes. Those summer days on the farm with my parents, siblings, and plenty of cousins, seemed to pass too fast.

Before we knew it, our Monday morning return arrived. My parents drove us to the station at 6 A.M. to catch the train back to Chicago. We said our sleepy goodbye. I gave Dad a hug. It was then I saw him take out his handkerchief and wipe tears from his eyes. The only other time I had seen him cry was when his mother died. We waved goodbye as we boarded for our last train ride to and from Dubuque. We never dreamed we were also saying goodbye for the final time to my Dad.

April 1985 Iowa Visit
Front: Maria (Spot)
Me, Eleanor, Joel, Gramma and
Grampa Freiburger

In the early hours of November 8th, 1985, the phone rang, and it was my sister-in-law calling to tell me that Dad had died suddenly during the night of a heart attack. He was 73, and seemingly in good health. I went out in the cold early morning and sat on the deck tearfully thinking of the long journey he and I had traveled from those early years when he had expectations of me as his successor on the farm. We had made our way through our differences when I was in high school. Hard as it must have been for him, he respected my decision to become a doctor. His devotion to the Catholic faith brought us closer together when I entered the seminary. He was at my side when I left the priesthood and when the time came, he proudly walked down the aisle with me when Eleanor and I wed. He traveled to Connecticut with my Mom for another proud moment when I received my PhD (I was a doctor after all.)

I thought back to his tears as we were boarding the train. Now my tears were a mix of sadness at the thought he was gone and for the sorrow I had caused him in my youth. But they were tears of thanks, too, as I thought back to sitting with him reviewing my college thesis, when he shared, "You may have left the farm, but you kept your roots." From then on he had supported all the turns of events in my life—right up to that last visit; his tears at the station were a sign of his love and pride in my becoming a parent.

I was honored that my siblings chose me to give his eulogy. I recalled our father as a man of faith, a custodian of the soil, and a father so worthy of respect and love. We celebrated his life in the Church that he, as a trustee, had helped to build. Fittingly ten clergy were present in the sanctuary to honor and thank him.

Bill McGheehan, who had moved from Manchester and had become a friend of Dad, attended the funeral Mass. Afterwards he came over, expressed his condolences, and said: "As I sat in church and listened, I realized a very important person was being honored." Bill's comments took me back to my youthful days when I saw Dad as a hero. His words softened my grief. Raphael Freiburger was, indeed, a hero, not only to me.

As a kid I had seen my Dad as a very important man, pictured on a calendar. That image was just that, a remarkably skilled and forward-looking farmer whose soil conservation practices were visually recognized by the John Deere Corporation. Over the years I came to know why he had been honored. Behind the photo was a man whose values are still thriving and guiding my life. The purpose of my odyssey is to live those values.

Chapter 43

The Odyssey Continues

I was starting yet another phase of my odyssey, developing a professional path. I felt, but did not fully realize, the void I wanted to fill after I left the priesthood. For eight years I had served in a pastoral leadership role. Couples turned to me to prepare for and witness their marriages. Families sought me out to baptize their babies, guide them in their challenges in and outside confession. And at the end of their loved ones' lives, they found some consolation in my being with them at the bedside to pray and offer the Sacrament of the Sick (then called extreme unction). I recall one parishioner summarizing my role, "I come to you when I have to make important life decisions." Now I was faced with finding a new way to fill that void.

I was searching for a leadership role in the public arena, unaware of what it would look like and how it would fill my void. The first opportunity to fill that void presented itself when as a high school biology teacher in Burlington in 1971. During the negotiations process that year, I had realized I needed new skills and a new approach.

In the University of Vermont graduate program, I began applying what I was learning in my teaching, committee assignments, and in the State Department of Education. During the next three years in Burlington, I became a father. I had no degrees or experience for that role.

In 1972, I had been invited to apply for doctoral studies in Educational Leadership at the University of Connecticut. After completing my doctoral studies, I had been hired as the director of a newly established Center of Community Education at Rhode Island College. The center's mission involved meeting with school districts and community members throughout the state, explaining community education—a unique planning process which brought together community agencies to utilize the school building as the site of providing services to community members. I designed my presentation in the same formal manner as my sermons. I was the "community education expert" who would make their schools and communities better places.

After one of my early presentations in the combined district of Foster-Glocester, Rhode Island, which I thought I had prepared for and delivered well, a Glocester school board member announced: "Community education will never work here. Our communities have long histories as separate identities, and there's no possibility of trying to get them to cooperate. You can tell a Foster student by the way he walks when boarding the school bus. We use separate buses for each town, and that's the way we have to do things here."

I was shocked, I'm not sure how I stumbled through an obviously inadequate answer, which abruptly ended the meeting. I left embarrassed, lacking an answer. I was not aware I did not need an answer.

I had gone to the meeting as an outsider full of assumptions about what a community needs and should do. I had slipped back to my priestly role when rules defined and spelled out "answers" about the way a program should work. Now I needed to question and listen to the community residents and help them explore and shape their own idea of a community school.

Driving home, I had a flashback to the farm. I thought of my father. He had been an entrepreneur in farming methods, and not everyone agreed with the way he farmed. I needed to go back to his patient approach of helping his neighbors understand and accept new ways of nurturing the soil. I remember one of the neighbors, after asking about strip cropping, told Dad that if he drove his tractor around strip cropping on his farm all day, all those turns would drive him to the "nut house." As we walked away Dad quipped, "I guess he thinks I'm already in the 'nut house'."

Community Education was a significantly different concept of "nourishing" a community by making the school its center. Foster-Glocester had to define what it needed and how to get there. In future presentations, I must be patient and open to the community members. The question I now would pose was, "How can schools become a place where the community chooses to come together to provide needed services that make this a better place to live?"

I began to see leadership in a new light. I could assist the community in taking ownership of their project. Lao Szu says it well, "When the work of the people is done, they will say 'We did it'."

Racism – Dealing with White Bias

Learning to lead by questioning, then carefully listening applied to other areas of bias in my past life that I had not yet recognized. Working with diverse community members helped me recognize how shielded I had been in my early years..

I had grown up in Asbury, Iowa, a small rural town of white families. When I was ten years old, we had visited my uncle Tom Sheean's farm in Shullsburg, Wisconsin. Tom had shown us a cement platform with a ring and chain attached. He told us it was used to chain slaves at night so they wouldn't run away, I asked, "Who were slaves?" For the first time I heard that "colored people" were slaves. Something was wrong. I felt sad and confused that people would be treated that way. I responded, "I hope there aren't any slaves today." That was the end of that discussion for many years.

In 1960 in the seminary, I would begin to understand why I felt confused and sad. I sat at breakfast with the renowned John Howard Griffin as he shared his shocking experiences in his book, *"Black Like Me."* Griffin had traveled a as a white journalist through the deep South. Then months later after dyeing his skin, he traveled as a black man. At each stop, he compared the reception he received as a white, then as a black man. His story was shocking.

Griffin explained that when he first looked at himself in the mirror, he came "face-to-face" with his own racism and had a hard time accepting his new black state, defining him solely by the color of his skin. I was stunned by his motivation and the description of his experiences. My sheltered existence, even in the seminary, prevented me from genuinely identifying with his experience.

In 1980, I was hired by a black owned management consulting firm, A.L. Nellum and Associates in Washington, D.C. I had pretty much forgotten that visit with John Howard Griffin and my lack of empathy for his horrific racist experience.

I co-directed a research project with Lelia Allen, a black woman. She invited me to join her one evening at a Fats Waller concert. When we entered the theater lobby, every eye focused on me, the only white man in the area. I felt so out of place, especially accompanying a black woman, that I wanted to find the nearest exit and escape. Lelia detected my nervousness and quipped, "How does it feel having everyone stare at you?" Her comment jolted me. My stomach knotted. That evening I started to understand what blacks experience every single day in our country's heavily dominant white culture.

Working with A.L. Nellum Associates often placed me as the only white person on the team. The following summer a black woman and I co-facilitated a weeklong workshop focused on racial biases. Each group was a mix of black and white participants. The purpose of the workshop was to help all attending to recognize hidden cultural biases and take positive steps to acknowledge and then change our behaviors.

During the workshop a 50-year-old white woman, whom I'll call Stella, casually shared two of her concerns with me: She was uncomfortable in discussions about prejudice and she felt the black participants were judging her as having white cultural bias. In the large group discussions during the week I noticed how she nervously shuffled her feet nervously when white biases were addressed.

On the last day of the workshop Stella called me aside and told me, "I was happy that a white person was a trainer. I don't think I would have been comfortable if the only trainers were black. While I understand the black participants felt they were rarely treated as equals, I'm sympathetic and I do support efforts to give them equal opportunities in the workplace. But I am a Daughter of the Confederacy and blacks will never be invited to be a part of the social circle in my home." I was struck silent.

Stella reminded me that cultural bias is the window through which we showcase our values. Her door remained shut and not even a week's worth of sessions had opened it a crack. I was happy that in the wrap up session, the trainees thanked us for creating an open forum to discuss racial issues and address positive steps they could take to combat bias. I returned to D.C. still questioning my own unconscious bias.

In 1986, when a family of South African refugees lived with Eleanor and me, we would spend long evenings trying to sort through layers of embedded biases. Living together as families, we shared our common human hopes and dreams—freedom, health, and opportunities for our children. I may have inched toward understanding my white privilege, but I had learned to acknowledge I had many miles to go in my internal odyssey.

CHAPTER 44

A Welcoming Home

When we moved to New Hampshire from Rhode Island, I continued developing skills and experiences I would need. in the future. Even though the job shifts from Rhode Island had gone smoothly for me, we all, especially Joel and Maria had challenging transitions. A new school, a new home, new kids in the neighborhood—all proved to be a very difficult uprooting. Home was now Belmont St. not Douglas Rd., and I arrived from work the first Tuesday to find five-year-old Maria standing outside by the curb with a suitcase packed with her belongings. She told me in her strongest defiant voice, "I'm going back to Rhode Island." After an hour in the cold, and lured inside by her favorite dinner, we talked about how she was feeling. Finally, she decided to stay in New Hampshire for a little longer.

Joel, too, had left behind an extraordinarily creative teacher with whom he had bonded He was now struggling to deal with a whole new environment. Fortunately, one of his new teachers spent time with him and gave him some special jobs in her classroom. It took time, but both kids did make new friends and gradually accepted the move. One night we overheard Joel asking Maria if she still missed Rhode Island. To our relief, she said, "No. I'm too busy!" Finally comfortable in our new home and neighborhood, we found our house becoming a hospitality center.

On the farm we always had a house full of visitors. Eleanor grew up working as a hostess and waitress. Her family's business motto, "Welcome, come as you are," applied to both of our families: mine, the farm; and hers, restaurants and hotels. Wherever we lived, she gathered the neighbors and planned activities. I always had the good fortune to be a part of the organizing role.

In Rhode Island, we watched the children, decked out in the most creative costumes, simply running from door to door collecting as much candy as possible. It was disappointing that after all the build up, Trick or Treating would be over in 20 or 30 minutes. So, Eleanor initiated a Halloween block party that continued for seven years. She also energized our Apponaug parish, directing two parish variety shows. The first had 150 and second had 200 parishioners on stage or behind the scenes. Before moving to Manchester, those parishioners and neighbors held a party and presented her with a framed collage of photos inscribed, "You came into our lives and we have grown."

Our annual Halloween block party "moved" to Manchester with us. Our home was party central, and all the neighborhood parents/grandparents invited their families (numbering between 75 and 135). The annual gathering, which existed before organizations created haunted houses and costumed events as fundraisers, was featured on the local tv station's, WMUR, evening news. We Belmont Street residents requested the city barricade our section of the street. One year the Greek Orthodox pastor, who lived in the neighborhood, dressed as the devil and led a two-block parade of goblins, pirates, witches, rotund walking pumpkins, and costumed adults. Every young person who marched in the parade went past every elderly neighbor's home. They returned to our yard for an award ceremony and received a ribbon for "the uniqueness" of his/her costume. I hosted the adults gathered in the garage serving our "annual must," Marie Harkinson's home made rum punch. It never failed to warm our innards and stimulate conversation.

Manchester Halloween Party

Ghostly music created a ghoulish atmosphere. There was a game for everyone: bobbing for apples, attempting, without using your hands, to eat donuts strung between the trees, trying to run sack races in costumes, and attempting a variety of other games. Older kids transformed a tacky woodshed into a creepy haunted house that even scared the parents. At the end of the day, all of us raised our ghoulish glasses of wine and toasted yet another successful Halloween, a celebration of many kids "favorite night."

Over its eight years, kids of all ages anticipated the block party. The local orthodontist shared his story with our daughter at one of her September morning appointments. He and his wife, Ellen, had told his family they'd be going to Disney World. There was great excitement until one of his kids realized the date: "But that's the weekend of the Freiburger Halloween party!"

"Now that's really something," Dr. Meehan said, "when a Halloween party can compete with a trip to Disney World!"

In addition to Halloween parties, while in Rhode Island, Eleanor also reached out to the larger community directing a statewide program, *Readers Anonymous*, which taught adults to read. Later in an adult education course for the disabled, she met Harold "Laddie" Holt. Physically handicapped with Cerebral Palsy, he only had control of his right foot. During his years confined to a wheelchair, he had conscientiously and persistently typed verse fragments and his life story, one letter at a time on a typewriter set on the floor. Eleanor collected the endless curled scrolls of his notes and created two books, *As I Am*, a collection of poems, and *In the Other Fellow's Shoes*, his autobiography in short stories. Before the 1990 vote on the Americans with Disabilities Act (ADA), Rhode Island Senator John Chaffee placed copies of Laddie's two books on the desk of every United States Senator. It had taken almost ten years to become the law of the land. Laddie justifiably felt that his years of toil and perspiration contributed to recognition and support for millions of disabled people.

Laddie's tireless efforts were also an example to us to apply in our Manchester neighborhood, a cross section of seniors, middle agers, students, youth, widowers and widows. Regularly, a team of neighbor friends and bakers, delivered at least three versions of coffee cake, bread, or cookies to those who lived alone. We caroled at their doors at Christmas time. We all took turns visiting aging neighbors throughout the year.

The spirit of hospitality extended to our Iowa families. The years when we made our annual visits to Iowa in the summer had passed. Now, we had the fun of having my siblings and their families come East. In the summer of 1985, my niece Kristen joined us and worked in a local restaurant. The Iowa connection continued, and nephews Paul and Eric spent a summer with us working on construction projects on Hanover Street in Manchester. Their stay reminded me of my days on the farm. Like my parents, we were hosting nieces and nephews as part of our family, deepening cousin ties that still remain.

During our careers we also had the great privilege – and fun – of expanding our global family, thanks to Southern New Hampshire University's international students. When interviewing at University of Notre Dame as a candidate for a role in Kenya in the summer of 1994, Maria was asked this question: "So, how will a young woman who grew up in 'lily white New Hampshire' deal with an entirely black community in Kenya?" Her response was, "Oh New Hampshire may be "lily white." But you should visit 1475 Belmont Street. On almost any day you'll find diversity."

Refugees from South Africa became part of the household. One evening as I arrived home, the garage door opened ahead of me. Eleanor was backing out the car with two passengers, students in the Community Economic Development (CED) program at Southern NH University. She rolled down the car window and introduced the South African refugees to me. Tshidi and Diana had received USAID scholarships to study in the US.

Tshidi had accepted a scholarship to Southern NH University even though she was pregnant with her third child. Her husband agreed to stay behind in a refugee camp in Africa with their four-year-old son, Rungulane. Tragically, their second child, a daughter, had died shortly after birth. A few weeks into the semester Tshidi explained to a professor that she had come to America pregnant. Both she and her husband felt it was important for her to take advantage of such an opportunity. But living in the dormitory, she was deeply concerned about her new baby following the death of her previous child. The professor approached Eleanor inquiring about finding a place for Tshidi to stay when she delivered her baby. We talked about this with our children, Maria, then in fifth grade and Joel, in eighth grade. They agreed that we should invite her to live with us. In April, 1986, Tshidi gave birth to healthy baby girl, Mpho (meaning "gift"). Mother and child came home to 1475 Belmont Street. Mpho returned from South Africa to live with us again in 2013.

A day later, our rather strait-laced neighbor wandered over to our yard when he saw me putting up pink balloons on our lamp post. "I didn't realize Eleanor was pregnant! Do you have a new baby?" "Yes, "I responded; we do have a new baby and she is black." Speechless, he turned, and walked home shaking his head incredulously and almost biting off the stem of his pipe. It was quite some time before we saw him again.

Eddie, Maria, Mpho, Umbatha, Tshidi, Rungulane and Me
1995

But Tshidi and Mpho weren't our only mother-daughter house guests. Shortly after Tshidi and Mpho moved to an apartment, another refugee from El Salvador and her baby daughter, Victoria, also joined us. On her 25th birthday she drove to Manchester with her mother to visit the home where she lived as a newborn.

Victoria and Virginia

In the morning on her way to CED classes, each mother would wrap her child and put her in a car seat. In the evenings Tshidi introduced us, firsthand, to the horrors of apartheid. Virginia did the same regarding her beloved El Salvador. We experienced home schooling at its best!

On another occasion, Sirikiat Praphailong and Visuthan Tantivanich, known to all as Joe and Apple, graduate students from Thailand, held their wedding reception in our backyard. I stood on a stepladder hanging Thai paper lanterns and other decorations with Apple's father. We converted our small backyard into "little Bangkok." I was honored at the dinner for sixty guests, to present a toast to the couple's future happiness. The moment had triple significance. The bride's sister and husband, as well as Eleanor and I, and now Joe and Apple, all shared August 7 as our wedding day. After the reception, the heavens opened in a huge rainstorm. Friends and family from ten countries gathered in our living room to watch the video of the wedding.

Maldivian student, Eemaan, whom Eleanor had taught at SNHU's Malaysian international campus, came to Manchester's campus to complete her degree. We learned so much about Islam and Maldivian culture when Eemaan lived with us. In 2010, she earned her Master's degree. Her father, Ibrahim Rameez, had traveled extensively in Europe and Asia, and Eemaan's sister, Noora, stayed with us for her graduation. Noora introduced us to Maldivian cuisine. One early morning while I was making pancakes for breakfast, Ibraham stepped outside and had his first cigarette of the day. When he returned to the kitchen he commented, "This is a different America than I see on CNN. Until I experienced what it was like to be at 'home' in New Hampshire, I never really knew what America was like."

Left to right: Back row: Me, Eleanor
Front row: Eemaan, Ibrahim, Noora

During those years the SNHU's tagline was, *Where the World Comes to Mind*. In those interesting years there was no doubt that the world had not only come to our minds, but to our home and family as well. Every one "came as they were" and left us better than we thought we could be. "Come in," was the welcoming call when they rang the doorbell at 1475 Belmont Street. Their presence warmed our home and hearts.

CHAPTER 45

Politics and the Workplace

In 1982, I transferred from my position at Parker House in Boston to the Sheraton Wayfarer in Bedford, New Hampshire. I had a year to prepare for my first ever lesson about the political process during the New Hampshire first in the Nation Presidential Primary. The Wayfarer was the host site the evening before Primary Day and the place pulsed with the Democratic presidential candidates, major supporters. and the national press. My insider's lens gave me a front row seat to watch these three groups interact.

The event was off the record, so the candidates were relaxed in their conversations. The CEOs of two major health insurance companies lobbied the poll leaders Gary Hart, John Glenn, Walter Mondale and Fritz Hollingsworth with an eye toward the next day's vote. The candidates were intent on seeking endorsements from *The Union Leader* and other local papers. The star attraction that evening was Jesse Jackson, the first viable African American candidate to run for the Presidency after Shirley Chisolm. Jackson attracted a New Hampshire crowd supporting his stand that acid rain was destroying NH forests. Reporters were peppering the candidates with questions about how they planned to beat Ronald Reagan in the general election. I listened to Walter Mondale, a mild-mannered Midwestern former Vice-President, trying to explain to reporters and the crowd gathered around him, his tax plan to help middle America. That evening's gathering was a workshop on how candidates frame and communicate their policies.

Primary Day, Tuesday, February 28, generated the excitement of a Big Top Circus. The parking lot behind the convention center was a maze of trailers and electrical wiring. The press featured newscasts with backdrops of the snowy banks of Goffe's Mill stream coursing under the Wayfarer's historic covered bridge. I watched CBS anchor Dan Rather in a barker role standing by the stream changing his wardrobe for three different updates of the primary returns. His assistants, with a whole rack of ties, attempted to match shirts, ties and suit jackets. From a temporary newsroom in the Wayfarer dining room, John Chancellor of the NBC network, reported trends and current voting totals.

After all the vote tallies were in and the exhausting activities of the day activities were wrapping up, I escorted ABC reporter Diane Sawyer and other members of the press over the covered bridge to their rooms. Each one, although totally exhausted, spoke of the excitement the primary created for the upcoming presidential race.

Along with the aroma of strong coffee filling the air the "morning after," the room buzzed with the candidates, their staff and press creating a mix of high notes and undertones. News people clustered around Gary Hart, the Primary winner. What was his stance on health care, acid rain, and other issues? Losing candidates, their staffs and reporters nursed their juice and coffee at corner tables and discussed their strategies for upcoming primaries. My behind-the-scenes proximity to this New Hampshire Primary was a Politics 101 course. But my job at the Wayfarer was a 24/7, and it was only later that I would apply the lesson as I approached the next stage of my odyssey.

When I became a human resources manager in banking a few years later, I realized my life involved more than just doing my job. Each day as I dropped off my kids at school, I drove past the fire station, the library, and other municipal agencies. Recognizing that my life depended on these and many other services, I wanted to expand my reach and make a difference in my family's well-being and in the lives of those in my community. I was now moving closer toward reaching my lifelong purpose.

Then as I was interviewing Alice, a candidate for an accounting job who was a single mom, she asked if the bank had a day care program for the children of employees. I had to say, no it did not. I named nonprofit centers in the city that did. The urgent tone in this excellent candidate's question prompted me to consider the importance of getting involved with agencies that made it possible for people like Alice to work for our bank. My workday at the bank did not involve the long days and nights I experienced at the hotel. I could now become involved with community needs.

In my role as a priest, I had a network I could tap into when caring for parishioner's needs. Now a resident of Manchester, a larger community, I began my search for boards and agencies who served the Alices and others like her. I joined Leadership Manchester, a program designed to introduce participants to the city's agencies and their services, including the local and state governments.

On one of our early morning tours of Manchester I saw homeless people waiting to enter a shelter for breakfast. What a wake-up call! I met David, an ex-Marine who had become homeless, leading him on a downward spiral and ultimately drug use. Two years later, when I joined the board of The Way Home, an agency dedicated to helping the homeless, especially veterans, I met David again, but not in a line of homeless vets waiting for breakfast. David had not only found his "Way Home," but a good job, thanks to the services provided by the nonprofit. As a fellow member on the Board, David would educate me about the complexity of his journey. Later I led a Way Home campaign to raise $250,000 in tax credits to rehab a house for homeless veterans.

I also joined the United Way Board and chaired the Allocations Committee, overseeing funding for community agencies. In this gratifying role, I worked with reviewers of grant awards to 33 agencies assisting the poor, youth, seniors and the homeless. After serving three years on the board, I was surprised and honored when named The United Way Volunteer of the Year. Walking back from the stage with the award, I thought to myself, "Thank you Mom and Dad for teaching me the importance of sharing with others."

While a board member of several other agencies, I experienced the encouraging work done by pastoral counselors. I relished the smiles on the faces of Latino students who received scholarships from a fund I inaugurated. And entrepreneurs were grateful for the assistance I offered when they developed business plans in the Amoskeag Business Incubator.

The combined experience in the hotel and banking industries and on non-profit boards, also raised my awareness of other critical issues like unequal pay for and failure to promote women to positions of responsibility in career paths, the importance of education in preparing students for the workforce, and the need for services to assist families, especially single moms.

Omni Hotels, my employer in the early 1980s, recognized the role of women and placed great emphasis on promoting them to leadership positions. Bank culture, on the contrary, was heavily male dominated, especially in higher paid roles. I remember asking a senior loan officer why he wasn't promoting a qualified woman. He answered, "She is a good lender, but businesses are run by men, and men don't listen to women." I pointed out the intent of the law on gender discrimination, but I could tell I wasn't getting through to him. When he left my office, I began to wonder how much impact one could have in an atmosphere so entrenched in gender bias.

I recalled lessons I had learned from the 1984 presidential primary. So many different groups had interacted to find ways to address the critical needs of people and the communities in which they live. When I was a community education director, I had attempted to help community members, schools, businesses, and agencies identify their needs. That experience had been my early eye-opener about developing the skills I needed to identify and find the resources to meet community needs.

In 1987, mistakenly feeling secure in my job, I also felt shackled and isolated. I thought about my role on nonprofit boards. So often in board meetings I would hear the executive director comment, "There are so many people we could help if we could just change the attitudes and biases blocking them." I was struck by the stark truth of the statement, and realized I needed to find a new path in my odyssey.

The opportunity came in September 1988. The dean of the New Hampshire College School of Business, now SNHU, invited me to apply for a position as a business professor. After Eleanor and I discussed this major career change, I recognized a college classroom would be an excellent setting to integrate many of my previous experiences.

I accepted a professorship teaching management and corporate social responsibility in the MBA program. That decision set me on a new "course" in my odyssey. For the next 20 years, I would learn from and teach students from all corners of the globe.

Chapter 46

New Hampshire College, Now Southern New Hampshire University

During two decades at Southern New Hampshire University (SNHU), I taught in some traditional classrooms here and abroad. I taught students of diverse cultures from 20+ countries, and often hosted students in our home for dinner and class meetings. They would bring a dish representing their country's cuisine and we would provide the American, Irish/German fare. To be sure our dishes were much less creative.

My graduate class, sharing ethnic food and discussing diverse ideas

I recall one evening, following dinner, one of the Pakistani students commented on the dress of Western women. The male students from Dubai, Pakistan, and Turkey, a majority in the class, challenged the women from Venezuela, Columbia and Brazil to explain how they saw the role of women and appropriate dress. When the women asked their fellow students why women wear Hijabs or Burkas, the Pakistani student said, "That's the way we interpret the

Quran; women's bodies should not be seen in public." The women contended: "Cultures evolve, and the dress of these women is degrading and makes them look like slaves to men." A lively debate ensued. I was intrigued hearing two different religiously based cultures try to struggle with women's role in society based on the issue of dress. Interestingly, the president of Pakistan at the time was a woman, Benazir Bhutto.

As I listened to their discussion, I had a flash-back to that earlier Foster-Glocester meeting. It had been an awakening and a turning point in my career. Now 30 years later sitting in my backyard, I was listening to my students discussing their different cultural understandings of a gender issue, and I realized that my odyssey had taken me a long unexpected way. I had grown by listening to and experiencing new cultures. I saw my own journey in my students now immersed and struggling with the same process.

Over the years I observed so many international students struggle to understand our American culture. I was fortunate to teach and live in Dubai and Greece, where, I too, would experience cultures that shaped my students' lives and work.

In my Dubai courses in 1996, I joined colleagues in a new delivery approach: distance education, now known as online education. This method used a hybrid model, a mix of face-to-face and online meetings.

In my first face-to-face meeting with 20 students in Dubai, I had a surprise. In the middle of the class period, the Muezzin called the hour of prayer. The students, in white sheikh clothing with head gear, unrolled their carpets and lay prone on the floor for prayer. I had read about the Muslim call to prayer before coming Dubai, but that had been "book learning." I was still in my American mindset, but on that evening I saw the deep respect my students had as they observed one of the Five Pillars of Islam. Seeing them in prayer reminded me of my own deep roots and religious prayers.

My Dubai stay also introduced me to Middle Eastern hospitality. Each student invited me to lunch and shared the story of his family and work. I recall sitting with Mohamet in the Dubai Chamber of Commerce as he described his Jihad pilgrimage studying the Quran in the desert. He proudly informed me he was chosen by his family to serve on a select committee, "planning to change Dubai from an oil economy to an international trade center." He elaborated, "Dubai law requires the Sheiks, the businessmen of the Dubai Muslim population, to own 51% of the businesses. In my opinion that will make the economic transition move faster." He made it a point to acknowledge that my course in corporate social responsibility had helped him with issues that arose in his committee work.

My student also introduced me to the Souk (marketplace) where I attempted to learn the art of bargaining and negotiating as a normal way of conducting business. The first time I tried to buy spices, I thought the merchant was asking the amount I wanted to buy. He kept shaking his head and saying, "Naah, Naah" and wagging his finger at me. Then my student started negotiating the cost and all went well. I gladly let him negotiate the remainder of my purchases. Being immersed in Arabic culture gave me so much more appreciation of its rich heritage while making me realize just how much I did not know.

I would have another cultural experience when I taught in Greece in 1998. In Athens, where I was teaching Organizational Behavior, the Greeks first applied the groundwork principles for participative management and ethics, the core of my courses.

On a walking tour to the Acropolis, we gathered in front of the remnant pillars of the Parthenon. I stared with the question: "Who is the greatest leader in Greek history?" I expected several names might surface, especially Alexander the Great who expanded Hellenism from India to Egypt.

But no! The very first response was, "Pericles." I asked why him?

"He is the father of democracy and gathered great minds like Socrates, the father of Philosophy."

Here I was, standing before the Parthenon using Socrates' own teaching method with my students. I realized the Greek historian, Thucydides, had foreseen Pericles and Socrates as legendary figures whose leadership and teachings would permeate thought for centuries. I was a student of their thought. I was reenacting their legacy in my Athenian classroom.

In 2001, Malaysia was the setting of a third international experience when Eleanor went to teach at the SNHU campus in

Klang. I flew to Malaysia the first week of September to visit her before my classes started back in Manchester.

When Cheryl Victor and Gabriel Wee had studied at SNHU in Manchester in the mid-90s, they were Eleanor's students. Cheryl's family had visited our home. Now, in their home country in 2001, we shared several wonderful reunions and an unforgettably, tragic event with the Victor family.

Me, Eleanor, Gabriel Wee, Cheryl Victor

On September 11, 2001, they had invited us to a birthday party in Kuala Lumpur. We had just started dinner at 8:45 P.M. Malaysian time, when a cousin newspaper reporter received mobile call that a plane had crashed into the World Trade Center Towers in New York. We sat horrified at the thought of such an accident—just as the caller shouted that another plane was crashing into the second tower. There, halfway across the world on a hotel wide screen TV, a world away from New York City, we saw the tragedy happening. The whole world experienced sorrow that day, and in the kindness and sympathy shown us as Americans, I began to realize that, despite differences in cultures, rituals, wardrobes, and languages, we all share the same humanity. Even worlds away from "home," I felt at home because our human bond was so evident that evening in Kuala Lumpur and in the traumatic days that followed.

During those years. I learned so much from my students. I encouraged my classes to try to see the world through one another's lenses. One day on the Manchester campus after class in which international students were enrolled, an American student confided to me, "This is my fourth class with international students, but it is the first time the professor created an atmosphere where getting to know and appreciate them and their culture was a priority."

Eleanor's SNHU international career focused on human rights, the campus association she advised for 19 years. She was SNHU's initial appointee to the University's first Endowed Chair in Business Ethics. In 2013, when the University awarded her an honorary doctorate, President Paul LeBlanc described her as "The Conscience of the University." Eleanor integrated her university work with that of Global Citizens Circle (GCC). In that role she brought world leaders and activists as commencement speakers and introduced students to Nobel Peace Prize winners and human rights activists from all over the globe. Our university careers fulfilled what was SNHU's tag line for many years: *Where the World Comes to Mind.*

After many stages, and decades of life changing experiences, I had, indeed developed a new world view and vision of life through the eyes of my wife, children, and students.

Now retired, I have time to appreciate the next generation of our family. I watch livestream or attend the Princeton, MA, academic and sports events of my three grandsons: Simon, Willem, and Jackson, reminiscing about past days when I watched them learn to read and dribble a basketball. Since their births, I have visited and kept up to date with my two granddaughters, Sophia and Emily, enjoying their "firsts" in Glen Ellyn, IL, and, in between, on FaceTime. We've made memories together building sandcastles and collecting sea glass and splashing in the ocean waves along the Atlantic seacoast in New Hampshire. I look back, with an overwhelming sense of love, gratitude, and pride which have marked the stages of this Iowa farm boy's odyssey.

Grandad with the five grandchildren setting off on their unique odysseys.
Front: Willem, Emily, Jackson; Back: Simon Me, Sophia
Rye Beach 2010

RETROSPECT

Exeter, New Hampshire

Coursing to Great Bay and the Atlantic Ocean, the rushing Exeter River mingles with the Swampscott tidal basin outside the window of our apartment. As I watch, I can see my life streaming in the narrow little spring fed creek on the farm where my parents raised me and my siblings.

But this time I am looking back just a few years. I am walking toward it with my grandchildren pointing out the farms with their strip cropping neighboring the path and telling them their Great Grampa always spoke of those strips as conserving his soil for the future. Those fields of strip cropping, a practice he initiated, were his dream and legacy. I talk about my mother who had planted new seeds and helped us kids dream about our lives. All seven of us went to college and became engineers, researchers, or teachers—planting new gardens.

My boyhood dreams led me on a personal odyssey through ever-broadening life paths. My parents' steadfast role-modeling nurtured my ability to dream. They had stood with me at every turn. Their values had prepared me for a life beyond those fenced fields of the farm.

Fifty years have passed, and I stand here with Eleanor, children, and grandchildren. I can see each grandchild's unique ripple that will become their own odysseys. I hope our values can strengthen and support them all through their own journeys.

When I changed course in my life and married Eleanor, we chose Dag Hammarskjold's quote for our

Eleanor and Jim 2017

life together: *"For all that has been, Thanks! For all that will be, Yes!"* In that mutual "yes" this Iowa farm boy continues to navigate the course of what appeared to be an impossible odyssey.